PUBLIC SPEAKING
in a Global Context

FIRST EDITION

John William Haas

University of Tennessee–Knoxville

HAYDEN
HM
McNEIL

Hayden-McNeil Sustainability

Hayden-McNeil's standard paper stock uses a minimum of 30% post-consumer waste. We offer higher % options by request, including a 100% recycled stock. Additionally, Hayden-McNeil Custom Digital provides authors with the opportunity to convert print products to a digital format. Hayden-McNeil is part of a larger sustainability initiative through Macmillan Higher Ed. Visit http://sustainability.macmillan.com to learn more.

Printed in the United States of America

10 9 8 7 6 5 4 3 2 1

ISBN 978-0-7380-4661-7

Hayden-McNeil Publishing
14903 Pilot Drive
Plymouth, MI 48170
www.hmpublishing.com

HaasJ 4661-7 W15

TABLE OF CONTENTS

COURSE SYLLABUS

Communication Studies 210: Public Speaking
University of Tennessee

DEPARTMENT OFFICE

293 Communications Building
(865) 974-0696
Website: *http://cmst.cci.utk.edu/*

Course Requirements and Policies

Welcome to Public Speaking! We believe that this course will provide you with a truly valuable college experience. Following the successful completion of the course, you will be a more effective speaker and you will be better able to evaluate the speeches of others.

Our goal in this course is to prepare you to develop, deliver, and evaluate public speaking in an increasingly diverse world. We seek to advance your understanding of the principles and processes of communicating effectively in public situations. The course is also designed to develop your public speaking skills. We plan to do this through a combination of assignments involving class discussions, speaking, listening, writing, and reading assignments. The course assignments are designed to build your skills and knowledge of public speaking as we progress through the semester. In addition, you will learn from others as they engage in public speaking. Upon successful completion of the course, you will have a basic understanding of the public speaking process and a clear understanding of your own speaking strengths and weaknesses. That understanding of your own strengths and weaknesses will offer you direction on how to continue to grow as a speaker.

Photo provided by John William Haas

COURSE OBJECTIVES

After completing this course, students should:

1. Possess an understanding of the communication process;

2. Possess an understanding of how to prepare, deliver, and evaluate speeches;

3. Possess an understanding of how to adapt speeches to diverse audiences;

4. Possess an understanding of how to develop and deliver speeches that include intercultural/international topics;

5. Demonstrate an understanding of the ethical responsibilities associated with public speaking;

6. Demonstrate the skillful use of communication in public speaking contexts; and

7. Demonstrate the capacity to manage speech anxiety.

SCHEDULE OF CLASSES AND ASSIGNMENTS

A daily class schedule will be provided by your instructor.

REQUIRED TEXT

Haas, J.W. (2015). *Public Speaking in a Global Context*. Hayden-McNeil.

WEBPAGE RESOURCES

School of Communication Studies:

http://cmst.cci.utk.edu/

School of Communication Studies public speaking link:

http://cmst.cci.utk.edu/content/oral-communication

- Click on the appropriate topic of interest (e.g., speech anxiety, choosing a topic, etc.)

Hodges Library:

http://libguides.utk.edu/speech210

- This link to Hodges Library appears as part of the general category Research Guides

STUDENT RESPONSIBILITIES

We seek to accomplish a great deal over the course of the academic term. In order to achieve the course objectives you must commit to:

Coming to Class Prepared

Communication Studies 210 is not a lecture course. Most of your time in class will be spent interacting with others. You are responsible for completing the assigned readings prior to class.

Attending Class

Class attendance is mandatory. Absences *will* affect your final grade:

- For M/W/F classes, you are permitted a total of three (3) absences for ANY reason, including sickness, funeral, personal emergency, school-sponsored event, etc. For a T/R class you are entitled to two (2) absences for ANY reason, including sickness, funeral, emergency, school-sponsored event, etc.

- Each additional absence, beyond the number permitted, will result in a reduction in your final grade.

Completing Assignments as Scheduled

All assignments must be completed as scheduled by your instructor. Major assignments such as speeches and exams are announced well in advance; a make-up will only be allowed in the case of a documented illness or family crisis and by the consent of your instructor.

Delivering Speeches that Follow the Guidelines Listed Below:

- Presentations are to be original and reflect thorough preparation.

- Use of others' ideas or words must be accompanied by appropriate citations.

- All speeches must be within the boundaries of good judgment and taste. If in doubt about what is appropriate, check with your instructor **before** the speech is delivered.

- You must adhere to all legal statutes governing the community and university. Illegal or hazardous items (drugs, firearms or other weapons, live animals, explosives, etc.) and potentially disruptive or dangerous activities (extracting snake venom, cleaning fish, etc.) are not permissible in the classroom as visual aids.

- You may not jeopardize the safety of any audience member.

PLAGIARISM

University's Honor Statement

"An essential feature of the University of Tennessee is a commitment to maintaining an atmosphere of intellectual integrity and academic honesty. As a student of the University, I pledge that I will neither knowingly give nor receive any inappropriate assistance in academic work, thus affirming my own personal commitment to honor and integrity."

"Students are responsible for any acts of plagiarism. Plagiarism is using the intellectual property or product of someone else without giving proper credit. The undocumented use of someone else's words or ideas in any medium of communication (unless such information is recognized as common knowledge) is a serious offense, subject to disciplinary action that may include failure in a course and/or dismissal from the university. Specific examples of plagiarism are:

- Using without proper documentation (quotation marks and a citation) written or spoken words, phrases, or sentences from any source;

- Summarizing without proper documentation (usually a citation) ideas from another source (unless such information is recognized as common knowledge);

- Borrowing facts, statistics, graphs, pictorial representations, or phrases without acknowledging the source (unless such information is recognized as common knowledge);

- Collaborating on a graded assignment without the instructor's approval;

- Submitting work, either in whole or part, created by a professional service and used without attribution (e.g., paper, speech, bibliography, or photograph)."

DIVERSITY STATEMENT

The School of Communication Studies recognizes and values diversity. Exposing students to diverse people, ideas, and cultures increases opportunities for intellectual inquiry, encourages critical thinking, and enhances communication and information competence. When all viewpoints are heard, thoughtfully considered, and respectfully responded to, everyone benefits. Diversity and fairness unite us with the wider professional and global community.

Description of Assignments

SELF-INTRODUCTION SPEECH

The overarching goal of this speech is to inform, not to persuade. The purpose of this assignment is to introduce yourself to the class by condensing the most important information about yourself into a short speech (approximately 2–3 minutes). This assignment will require you to prepare the speech in advance—it is not an impromptu presentation.

IMPROMPTU SPEECHES

The overarching goal of this speech will be determined by your teacher, and that goal may be to inform or to persuade.

Many speaking situations you encounter in life will be impromptu. That is, you will be required to speak with little or no preparation. The impromptu speech requires the speaker to structure his or her thoughts quickly. This can be done with the use of a "template" or framework that you will learn over the course of the term.

When this assignment is made, the instructor will give you a few moments to gather your thoughts and prepare a few notes for use during the speech. Keep in mind that organization is the key to communicating your message and enhancing your credibility with the audience. For this kind of speech, seek to have a conversation with the audience and respond to their nonverbal feedback.

INFORMATIVE SPEECH ON INTERNATIONAL TOPIC

The overarching goal of this assignment is to inform. You must not engage in persuasion.

The purpose of this speech is to inform the audience about a concept, process, or event that involves an international or intercultural topic. Informative speeches are designed to bring new information to the audience. Consider your own interests and abilities when selecting the topic but also consider the kinds of topics that would be interesting to your audience.

You will need to use at least three (3) credible and current sources for this speech. You may use sources from the Web if the following information is available:

- The author's name and credentials (researcher, physician, college professor, etc.);

- The sponsoring organization (e.g., Mayo Clinic, The Centers for Disease Control and Prevention, etc.); and

- The date the information was reported on the website.

If information about the author or sponsoring organization is not available, this source should not be used for the assignment.

Informative Speech Outline
On the day you are scheduled to deliver the informative presentation, you must turn in a complete speech outline along with a list of references. Your outline must follow the format described in the text.

Time
You must complete the speech in the time allotted. Speeches significantly under or over the allotted time will incur a loss of points from the final grade. Speakers who exceed the allotted time may be stopped by the instructor.

Style of Delivery
Reading the speech is not permitted. A speaker who reads his/her presentation will fail the assignment. When you deliver your presentation, we expect you to be organized, make use of a speaking outline, and maintain eye contact with the audience. In addition, we expect you to make appropriate use of visual aids.

PERSUASIVE SPEECHES
You will be assigned to deliver two persuasive speeches over the course of the semester. The overarching goal of this assignment is to persuade. Note that you may also pursue an informative objective as part of this assignment. You may need to inform the audience about some aspect of your topic prior to introducing the persuasive objective.

The goal of these assignments is to prepare and deliver a speech designed to change or reinforce the attitudes, beliefs, and/or behaviors of the audience. You may wish to consider Monroe's Motivated Sequence as an organizational pattern for a persuasive speech of question of policy and a topical pattern for speeches of question of fact or value.

Persuasive Speech Outline

A copy of your speech outline and a list of sources must be turned in to your instructor at the beginning of the class session that you are scheduled to speak.

For each persuasive speech, you must include at least **five (5)** current and credible sources on your outline with a reference page attached. You may use sources from the Web if the following information is available:

- The author's name and credentials (researcher, physician, college professor, etc.);

- The sponsoring organization (e.g., Mayo Clinic, The Centers for Disease Control and Prevention, etc.); and

- The date the information was reported on the website.

Delivery Style

Reading the speech is not permitted and will result in failure for the assignment. When delivering each of these speeches, we expect you to be organized, make use of a speaking outline, and maintain eye contact with the audience. In addition, you are expected to make appropriate use of visual aids.

EXAMINATIONS

All students enrolled in Communication Studies 210 are required to take a Midterm and Final Exam. The examinations will be comprised of objective questions in multiple choice and true/false format. The Midterm will involve the material covered in the first half of the course; the Final Exam will cover the material discussed in the second half of the course.

LIBRARY ASSIGNMENT

Your class will receive a broad overview of library services relevant to public speaking prior to the informative speech assignment. The library session will center on the search engines and databases that are most helpful when searching for sources to support your speech objectives. Additional information about the library assignment will be covered in class.

RESEARCH PARTICIPATION

Each student will have the opportunity to participate in two (2) research projects during the course of the semester. This assignment supports research projects designed to explore effective communication. Your instructor will provide you with complete instructions on how to register for research participation credit. If you elect not to participate in research activities for any reason, your instructor will have available an alternative assignment for you to earn the research participation portion of your grade.

McCLUNG SPEECH CONTEST EVALUATION

Each semester, CMST 210 students participate in the McClung Public Speaking Contest sponsored by the School of Communication Studies. All public speaking students are eligible to participate and cash prizes will be awarded to the winners. As you plan your informative speech on an international topic this term, keep the contest in mind.

One student from each section of CMST 210 will represent his or her classmates in the competition. Each section will be responsible for selecting its representative. Talk to your instructor if you are interested in representing your section for this competition. Your instructor may select the representative or the class may vote on its representative.

There will be two rounds of speeches (a preliminary round and a final round) and, if selected, you must be available to present on both dates. The dates for the preliminary round and the final round will be announced in class. The top five speakers from the preliminary round will progress to the final round. All final round speakers will receive a cash award. If you are not chosen to compete in the final round, you are required to attend the final round of the competition to complete the evaluation assignment.

Criteria for Grading Speeches

All CMST 210 instructors follow the same guidelines when grading speaking assignments. In general, a "C" on a speech means that you have met the minimum requirements for that assignment; a grade of "A" or "B" means that you have exceeded the minimum requirements in a significant way; and a grade of "D" or "F" means that you have failed to meet two or more of the requirements for the assignment.

THE AVERAGE GRADE FOR MAJOR SPEECHES IN THIS CLASS IS A C+

Simply attempting to deliver a scheduled speech does not guarantee that you will be assigned a passing grade. The criteria for assigning speech grades appear below:

1. **C = Average, satisfactory work**. To be judged as average and satisfactory, your work must:

   a. Meet all specific requirements for the assignment (length, purpose, organization, sources, delivery, etc.)

   b. Be delivered on the assigned date and within the appropriate time limit

   c. Exhibit sound organization—a clear purpose adequately supported by main ideas that are easily identified

   d. Be intellectually sound in developing a topic of worth with adequate and dependable supporting materials

   e. Fulfill any special requirements of the assignment—such as use of three examples of supporting material

   f. Exhibit reasonable directness and communicativeness in delivery

   g. Be correct in grammar, pronunciation, and articulation

Photo provided by John William Haas

2. **B = Above average work**. To be judged as above average, your work must meet the criteria for a "C" speech as well as the following:

   a. Exhibit skillful use of connectives/transitions

   b. Demonstrate above average skill in using language, organization, and supporting materials to engage and challenge the audience

   c. Establish genuine rapport and interaction with listeners through style and delivery

   d. Challenge the audience to think or arouse in listeners a depth of response

3. **A = Superior work**. To be judged superior, your speech must meet the criteria for a "C" and "B" speech, as well as the following:

   a. Constitute a genuinely individual contribution to the audience's thinking

   b. Demonstrate exceptional skill in using the communication elements to create audience understanding and acceptance of a complex viewpoint or argument

   c. Illustrate skillful mastery of connectives/transitions and of presentation of ideas

4. **D or F = Below average work**. To be judged below average means that the speech is deficient in some or several of the factors required for an average "C" speech. **Any speech that is read will receive an F for that assignment. In addition, a speech that fails to meet the required number of sources for that assignment will not receive a grade above a C.**

COMMUNICATION AND PUBLIC SPEAKING OVERVIEW

CHAPTER 1

INTRODUCING PUBLIC SPEAKING

CHAPTER OBJECTIVES

This chapter is designed to help you understand:

- Your connection with public speaking

- The impact of public speaking in a global environment

- The ethics of public speaking

- Your responsibilities as a speaker

- The role of listening in the public speaking process

Photo provided by John William Haas

Speeches are a common part of our daily life. We experience speeches as part of our civic life, in the workplace, in places of worship, and in educational settings. What's more, we experience speeches in various contexts such as in person, on television, and in other mediated forms such as on a computer or other electronic devices. Quite literally, you have been exposed to thousands of speeches over the course of your lifetime. Despite the number of speeches people experience, public speaking remains something of a puzzle. For many people, there is not a clear understanding of how to prepare and deliver a speech effectively. In addition, evaluating the speeches of others remains a problematic issue for audience members.

Consider the following questions. What makes a person an effective public speaker? What makes a person an ineffective public speaker? How can a speaker communicate well with diverse populations? More generally, why should you be concerned with public speaking? We will seek to answer these questions in the following pages and provide direction on how you can become a more effective public speaker.

STEVE JOBS AND THE SPOKEN WORD

Steve Jobs is *still* the world's greatest corporate storyteller. I've seen plenty of talented speakers in the past year and I've written about many of them in this column but I have yet to find someone as good as Steve Jobs. This is why I have spent so many years reviewing, analyzing and sharing Jobs' presentation techniques because leaders and entrepreneurs today need to carry on his legacy if we hope to inspire the world with our ideas. His keynote presentations continue to attract thousands of views on YouTube and he has profoundly impacted the way leaders communicate.

—Carmine Gallo, *Forbes*

Your Connection with Public Speaking

Many people believe that public speaking will play little, if any, role in their life. They do not plan to pursue an occupation that might involve speeches such as the ministry or elective office. As a consequence, many people do not expect (or desire!) to deliver speeches outside of the classroom. Moreover, few of us even consider attending an event devoted to speeches. Think about it—when was the last time you and your friends talked about going out to see a speech?

Simply put, we have a much stronger connection with public speaking than most people realize. Take the opportunity over the next week to count the number of times you are exposed to a speech. You will experience speeches delivered in class, at work, or through the media. You may be surprised by the number of speeches that you encounter during an average week. To clarify, your connection with public speaking will impact you in the following ways.

First, you are a **consumer of messages**. When we consume messages, they have an impact on us. Our attitudes, behaviors, and expectations are influenced by what others say to us. Speeches create an opportunity to influence message consumers. This kind of opportunity for a communicator is relatively rare. There simply are not many other contexts in which one person has the attention of many for an extended time.

Following the completion of this course, you will continue to be exposed to speeches on a regular basis. When attending music awards shows or political campaigns or graduation ceremonies, you will encounter speeches. Moreover, speeches are delivered in most every workplace on a routine basis. Speakers will, in your lifetime, have thousands of opportunities to influence everything about you, from your religious beliefs to your political attitudes to your entertainment preferences. However, not one of us was born with an understanding of how to assess the worth of a speech. We learn how to weigh the content of a speaker's message. We learn how to judge the quality of the speaker's delivery. Moreover, we learn how to assess the worth of a speech within a cultural context. This course may provide one of the few opportunities that you will ever have to systematically study public speaking.

Second, you are a **producer of messages**. When we produce messages, we seek to influence the attitudes and behaviors of others. You produce messages in many contexts—in interpersonal settings, in group settings, in organizational settings, or in public settings. In each of these settings you will have the opportunity to impact others. However, few opportunities will offer you the potential to influence the opinions of others as readily as a speech. Speeches provide a context in which people gather with the express purpose of listening to one speaker. Building on the skills and knowledge that you master from this course, you will become a more effective, more confident producer of messages.

Regardless of the context, there are many commonalities in the ways we produce messages. Many of the things we do to produce effective messages in interpersonal settings are similar to the ways we produce effective speeches. While most all of us have been taught to speak, few people have had systematic instruction that centers on how to speak well. Public speaking is part art, part science. The principles that underlie public speaking can be learned and, through practice, applied effectively.

Speaking Ethically

What does it mean to be an effective speaker? For centuries, the answer to that question always included some mention of ethics. In fact, one common understanding of an effective communicator was best described as "The Good Man Speaking Well." This phrase is generally credited to Cato the Elder who was born in Tusculum, Italy in 234 B.C. This idea is noteworthy because it expresses clearly the belief that ethical conduct and effective speaking are inseparable (Murphy, Katula, and Hoppmann, 2013). In this section, we will consider the ethical implications of your messages and their impact on the audience.

Simply put, messages have effects. As a speaker, your messages have the potential to influence the thinking and behaviors of others. In this course, we will expect you to examine closely the ways your messages might influence receivers as well as the consequences associated with changing the receivers' thoughts and behaviors. Unethical public speaking means that the speaker does not conform to the values and beliefs that are part of our culture about how we should treat others. Consider the following:

- When, if ever, is it acceptable for a speaker to mislead an audience?

- When, if ever, is it acceptable for a speaker to achieve his/her objectives at the expense of audience members?

- When, if ever, is it acceptable for a speaker to influence others when they do not wish to be influenced?

- When, if ever, is it acceptable to attack a person in a speech rather than attack the ideas that person holds?

- When, if ever, is it acceptable for a speaker to call on an audience to do harm to others?

Ethics deals with questions about the meaning of good and evil as well as right and wrong (Nilsen 1974; Pearson, Child, Mattern, and Kahl, 2006). Ethics can be defined as a **set of standards for conduct and moral judgment**. As consumers and producers of messages, we use ethical guidelines to assess speeches in terms of truthfulness, fairness, and credibility.

A QUESTION OF ETHICS

The belief that ethics and public speaking are linked is older than Cato. Plato considered this idea 200 years prior to Cato. However, it may be that the ancient Egyptians first began teaching students principles of both good behavior and good speech around 2,200 B.C. (Fox, 1983).

You now share a connection with students from 4,000 years in the past. Like you, they were expected to speak effectively and ethically in public speaking settings.

Once integrity goes, the rest is a piece of cake.

— J.R. Ewing, lead character in the 20th-century American television show *Dallas*

Josephson Institute

Ethics are important in public speaking because of the power of the spoken word. Nothing spells success more in life than the power of public speaking. Those who can fluently get their message across to an audience in a way that is impactful and memorable stand to achieve goals that are professional and personally satisfying. While skillful speaking has the power to positively impact others, few would dismiss the power of a speech to harm.

SOCIAL RESPONSIBILITY

A speaker has a duty to use the power of the spoken word responsibly. As an individual in the U.S., you have the right to express yourself as guaranteed by the First Amendment of the Bill of Rights. It reads, "Congress shall make no law abridging the freedom of speech, or of the press." However, this right is not without limits. For example, you may not engage in speech that poses a **clear and present danger** to others. Supreme Court Justice Oliver Wendell Holmes summed up this limitation well in 1919 with his opinion that freedom of speech does not allow a speaker to endanger the safety of others by yelling "fire" in a crowded theatre where no fire exists. Eventually the standard used by the Supreme Court to judge a speech was modified in 1951 to include speech that is a **clear and probable danger**. That is, if a speech did not result in immediate, direct harm to others but has the tendency to bring about harm then it was judged to be unlawful speech. For example, a speech advocating the overthrow of the U.S. government might be judged not to be a direct danger but may have the tendency to cause harm to the nation.

In addition to using speech to endanger others, public speakers are ethically and legally bound to refrain from using fighting words and hate speech. In 1942, the Supreme Court (*Chaplinksy v. New Hampshire*) ruled that there is a category of face-to-face epithets, or "fighting words," that is wholly outside of the protection of the First Amendment: those words "which by their very utterance inflict injury."

The ethical standards that you follow in the public speaking process can be extended to other communication settings outside of the classroom. In fact, you use them to judge what you hear going on around you on a day-to-day basis. Although other communication contexts generally do not have the reach of public speaking, all communication contexts (e.g., interpersonal, group, etc.) provide a setting in which people seek to change something about the receivers by altering their understanding of a topic, reinforcing existing attitudes, and creating new attitudes. The intent to influence others carries with it a significant responsibility.

INDIVIDUAL RESPONSIBILITY

Just as a single speaker can do harm to groups of people or entire nations, a single speaker has the potential to harm individuals. Public speakers have a responsibility to individuals who are talked about in a speech. In some cases, there are responsibilities that are covered by law. For example, a speaker that falsely calls a person a thief or a murderer and, as a result, unjustifiably hurts that person's reputation commits slander. According to the laws of the state of Tennessee, slander is a form of defamation that results when a false and defamatory statement is spoken about a person (as opposed to written about a person). Slander results in injury to the person's character or reputation. Slander does not occur just because the statement is annoying, offensive, or embarrassing to a person; the statement must reasonably hold the person up to public hatred, contempt, or ridicule.

To ensure that you conform to the law and act as an ethical speaker, consider the following:

- Address ideas, not individuals. When debating the worth of an idea or position on an issue, focus on the ideas rather than the qualities or characteristics of any person who is mentioned in the speech.

- Avoid personal attacks. When others produce messages that are disagreeable or resort to name-calling, a human tendency is to respond in kind. Name-calling tends to generate emotional responses. That is, if you start name-calling, I'll respond with a few names of my own! Speeches often involve topics that are controversial such as health care policies or gun rights. Speakers pay a price for personal attacks—they are no longer viewed as ethical, credible sources.

- Be factually correct. A speaker is ethically bound to check his or her facts and make certain that the information covered in the speech is accurate. Regardless of how much or how little assistance a speaker receives in preparing the speech, it is ultimately the speaker who is responsible for the content of the speech.

- Maintain commitments. Do not share information in a speech that you have committed to keep private. Breaking a confidence in a speech is an unethical act.

RESPECTING THE WORK OF OTHERS

Information is very easy to come by in a highly interconnected world. It is often tempting to borrow the work of someone else for use in a speech. The example displayed in the text box highlights the ease with which information can be "borrowed" but also the ease with which the true source of the ideas can be revealed.

Taking the words or ideas of others and passing them off as your own is plagiarism. One of the criteria for an effective speech is to provide support for the position taken by the speaker. However, letting your audience know where you got your information is just as important, and avoids the problem of plagiarism. In addition, it is unethical to take the information out of context or twist the meaning of the original author(s).

The National Communication Association has proposed an ethical credo that lays out what counts as ethical communication. Those principles follow and may be found at the URL located below the statement.

IT WORKED FOR MICHAEL DOUGLAS

In politics, the old ones are the best.

Giving a speech in Canberra, Anthony Albanese, the Australian transport minister, launched an attack on Tony Abbott, the Liberal party opposition leader.

'In Australia we have serious challenges to solve and we need serious people to solve them,' he said. 'Unfortunately, Tony Abbott is not the least bit interested in fixing anything. He's only interested in two things—making Australians afraid of it and telling them who's to blame for it.'

If you think that sounds a tad familiar, you'd be right.

In the 1995 movie *The American President*, President Andrew Shepherd, played by Michael Douglas, tore into his rival Bob Rumson.

'We have serious problems to solve and we need serious men to solve them,' Shepherd said. 'And whatever your particular problem is, friend, I promise you, Bob Rumson is not the least bit interested in solving it. He is interested in two things and two things only—making you afraid of it and telling you who's to blame for it.'

—Toby Harnden, *Daily Mail Online*

NATIONAL
COMMUNICATION
ASSOCIATION

NCA Ethical Credo

"Questions of right and wrong arise whenever people communicate. Ethical communication is fundamental to responsible thinking, decision making, and the development of relationships and communities within and across contexts, cultures, channels, and media. Moreover, ethical communication enhances human worth and dignity by fostering truthfulness, fairness, responsibility, personal integrity, and respect for self and others. We believe that unethical communication threatens the quality of all communication and consequently the well-being of individuals and the society in which we live. Therefore we, the members of the National Communication Association, endorse and are committed to practicing the following principles of ethical communication:

- We advocate truthfulness, accuracy, honesty, and reason as essential to the integrity of communication.

- We endorse freedom of expression, diversity of perspective, and tolerance of dissent to achieve the informed and responsible decision making fundamental to a civil society.

- We strive to understand and respect other communicators before evaluating and responding to their messages.

- We promote access to communication resources and opportunities as necessary to fulfill human potential and contribute to the well-being of families, communities, and society.

- We promote communication climates of caring and mutual understanding that respect the unique needs and characteristics of individual communicators.

- We condemn communication that degrades individuals and humanity through distortion, intimidation, coercion, and violence, and through the expression of intolerance and hatred.

- We are committed to the courageous expression of personal convictions in pursuit of fairness and justice.

- We advocate sharing information, opinions, and feelings when facing significant choices while also respecting privacy and confidentiality.

- We accept responsibility for the short- and long-term consequences for our own communication and expect the same of others."

https://www.natcom.org/uploadedFiles/About_NCA/Leadership_and_Governance/Public_Policy_Platform/PDF-PolicyPlatform-NCA_Credo_for_Ethical_Communication.pdf

The University of Tennessee also maintains a policy regarding plagiarism that provides specific guidance on what it means to be an ethical, competent speaker. The Honor Statement provides specific examples of what constitutes plagiarism and appears on the following page. It may be found at http://catalog.utk.edu/content.php?catoid=1&navoid=156#hono_stat.

UT Honor Statement

Each student is responsible for his/her own personal integrity in academic life. While there is no affirmative duty to report the academic dishonesty of another, each student, given the dictates of his/her own conscience, may choose to act on any violation of the Honor Statement. Each student is responsible for knowing the terms and conditions of the Honor Statement and may acknowledge his/her adherence to the Honor Statement by writing "Pledged" and signing each graded class assignment and examination.

Students are also responsible for any acts of plagiarism. Plagiarism is using the intellectual property of someone else without giving proper credit. The undocumented use of someone else's words or ideas in any medium of communication (unless such information is recognized as common knowledge) is a serious offense, subject to disciplinary action that may include failure in a course and/or dismissal from the university.

Specific examples of plagiarism are:

- Copying without proper documentation (quotation marks and a citation) written or spoken words, phrases, or sentences from any source.

- Summarizing without proper documentation (usually a citation) ideas from another source (unless such information is recognized as common knowledge).

- Borrowing facts, statistics, graphs, pictorial representations, or phrases without acknowledging the source (unless such information is recognized as common knowledge).

- Collaborating on a graded assignment without instructor's approval.

- Submitting work, either in whole or part, created by a professional service and used without attribution (e.g., paper, speech, bibliography, or photograph).

CITING SOURCES
Throughout the semester, follow the directions below for citing.

- **Direct quotations:** These should be acknowledged in your speech or presentation either as "And I quote…" or "As [the source] put it…"

- **Book:** Include title and author: "In her book, *Democracy Through the Ages*, Joy Hart stated…."

- **Periodical/Magazine:** Include title and date: "As reported in the April 4, 2014 edition of *The Economist*, mortgage interest rates have…."

- **Journal:** Include journal title, date, and author: "According to an article by Bob Gwynne that appeared in the January 2014 edition of *Harvard Business Review*, recent polls indicate…"

- **Website:** For a website that is operated by an organization, include the company/organization name: "The University of Tennessee's website includes information…" For a news organization, use the organization's name and date: "NPR.com reported on July 2, 2013…"

- **Interviews, lecture notes, or personal communication:** Include the name and credentials of source: "John Scheb, a professor of Political Science at the University of Tennessee, stated…"

EXERCISE

You may be thinking, this sounds pretty clear but I'm still not sure what to do with actual statements. It may be helpful at this point to practice with examples of statements to determine what is ethical and what is unethical for a speaker in regards to citing sources. Complete the exercise found at the end of this chapter entitled "Plagiarism Exercise" and bring your responses to class for discussion.

Listening Ethically and Effectively

Your first thought as you read the heading above may have been to question what listening has to do with public speaking. Listening skills are not readily understood as a part of the public speaking process. To listen well, a person must understand the difference between hearing and listening. In addition, receivers must manage successfully the many listening barriers that exist in public speaking situations. As the textbox suggests, there are many things in our environment that compete for the attention of receivers.

Effective, ethical speakers are, first and foremost, effective listeners (Brownell, 2013). Only when we attend to the messages of the other parties involved in the interaction can we determine how to develop messages adapted to their understandings. As a student in a public speaking course, you will take on two separate but equally important roles: the role of speaker and the role of audience member. This means that you need to learn how to listen to and evaluate the speeches of others ethically and effectively.

LISTENING DEFINED

It is common to ask others if they are listening or to encourage others to listen. What is less common is an understanding of what takes place when people engage in listening. What is listening?

Surprising to some, there is quite an extensive list of things that people do when they listen. For example, people hear, interpret, evaluate, and respond when they engage in listening. For the purpose of this class, we will define **listening** as a process that involves hearing, evaluating, and responding to verbal and nonverbal messages (Floyd, 1985).

People listen for a variety of reasons, such as the need to gather information, demonstrate empathy, to be entertained, to be polite, or for the purpose of accepting or rejecting a message. Keep in mind, however, that hearing a message is not the same as listening to a

---

WHAT DID SHE JUST SAY?

Smart phones. Texting. Social networking. Tablets. Instant messaging. Email.

According to a 2012 Pew survey, 67 percent of cellphone owners found themselves checking their phone for messages, alerts or calls—even when they didn't notice their phone ringing or vibrating; and 29 percent of cellphone owners described their phone as "something they can't imagine living without."

We allow mindlessness to take precedence over the insight that strangers—that any of us—can offer each other. We're looking down at our phones when we could be looking up at all there is to see—you can't express facial expressions, body language and sarcasm in an email.

—Allie Caren,
National Public Radio

message. Moreover, listening does not mean compliance with the speaker's wishes. That is, I can listen well and not go along with the request of the speaker. Hearing involves the reception of sound by the eardrum. Listening involves the interpretation and understanding of the message and, hopefully, the retention of the message.

TYPES OF LISTENING

Are you aware that there are different types of listening? We listen differently depending on our objective in the situation. While a number of different types of listening have been identified, we will concentrate on five types that are most relevant to public speaking—discriminative, comprehensive, empathic, analytical, and appreciative.

Discriminative Listening

Discriminative listening involves the most basic kind of listening. Simply put, discriminative listening takes place when a person differentiates or discriminates between the sounds that are being received. For example, the sound that you make saying aloud "potato" is different from the sound made saying aloud "tomato." We learn to produce and receive nuanced sounds early in life. However, the process of listening for and discriminating between nuanced sounds in one language makes it difficult to speak other languages well because of challenge associated with mastering a new set of nuanced sounds.

Comprehensive Listening

This type of listening enables the receiver to determine the overall meaning the speaker is attempting to convey. When engaged in comprehensive listening, a receiver is focused on an accurate understanding of the speaker's message (both the verbal and nonverbal parts of the message).

In order to bring about a successful speech, both the speaker and the audience must engage in this type of listening. When engaging in this type of listening, the speaker is able to accurately arrive at an understanding of the audience response to the speech. Comprehensive listening on the part of the audience brings into focus what the speaker means to convey.

Empathic Listening

When we engage in empathic listening, we seek to demonstrate compassion for the speaker and understand how that person feels. We are not trying necessarily to be sympathetic but instead listen with the goal of feeling how the speaker feels. This requires the listener to attend closely to the nuanced emotional signals sent out by the speaker. Empathic listening is most often associated with special occasion speeches such as memorial services or graduation ceremonies.

Empathy and empathic listening are not limited to receivers, however. Speakers also engage in empathic listening in pursuit of persuasive or informative goals. For example, former *Today Show* host Ann Curry delivered the commencement address at Wheaton University calling

LISTENING AND SPEAKING WITH EMPATHY

Can a spark of empathy once ignited—however briefly, however tenuously—lead to reasoned decisions and to compassionate policies that might transform our world, including the precincts in which we live, into one in which there are fewer tragedies or less brutal echoes of them?

—Paul Farmer, addressing 2013 graduating class at the University of Delaware

upon the graduating class to exhibit greater empathy toward others (see http://www.youtube.com/watch?v=3Ieykyp160c). In a similar vein, physician and anthropologist Paul Farmer urged graduating seniors at the University of Delaware in 2013 to make use of empathetic listening as a path to reasoned action.

Analytical Listening

Analytical listening, as the name implies, focuses on evaluation of a message. Engaging in this type of listening calls on the receiver to weigh the merit of the speaker's message. This type of listening requires immediate effort by the receiver to assess the message and relate it to other parts of the speech. Listening in this fashion tests the critical thinking skills of receivers.

We sometimes hear audience members make statements such as, "I was listening for…" With analytical listening, the receiver is listening for facts, statistical data, and other forms of evidence in support of the speaker's position. Acceptance or rejection of the speaker's message hinges on whether the ideas and positions are analytically sound.

Appreciative Listening

Appreciative listening focuses on the entertainment needs of the receiver. For example, listening to the inspiring words of a speaker or the music from your favorite musical artist stimulates you to engage in appreciative listening. Appreciative listening in public speaking contexts often takes place during special occasion speeches involving events such as award ceremonies or wedding toasts. In fact, if you have ever enjoyed a night out at a comedy club, then you engaged in appreciative listening.

LISTENER RESPONSIBILITIES—EFFECTIVE LISTENING

Listeners have a responsibility to behave ethically in public speaking situations. Effective, ethical listening requires the receiver to be actively engaged in the public speaking process. The listener shares with the speaker a responsibility for successful communication. When participating as a member of the audience, you are expected to give the speaker your undivided attention. In addition, you should listen for:

- The speaker's objectives;

- The main ideas and the relationships among these ideas;

- The claims made by the speaker (e.g., "All of the members of the other party believe…");

- Bias and/or prejudice;

- Statements of fact and statements of opinion; and

- The reasoning used by the speaker.

Causes of Poor Listening

We know that people often experience difficulty with the listening process. Brownell (2013) identified a number of **filters** that present barriers to effective listening. Specifically, these filters include:

- The setting (heat, light, noise, and time of day)

- Receiver interests

- Receiver values

- Receiver assumptions

- Receiver bias

- Receiver background and experiences

- The emotional state(s) of the receiver(s)

When you consider all of the filters that messages must pass through, it is quite an accomplishment to listen effectively. Some, or all, of the following may present you with listening difficulties.

- **Lack of interest.** If receivers have little or no interest in the topic, listening well will be a challenge. Unfortunately, listeners with no interest in the speech often distract both the speaker and other receivers with inappropriate nonverbal behaviors such as expressions of boredom. Expressions of boredom are generally interpreted by others as a sign of disrespect.

  When you find that you have little or no interest in the topic, consider carefully other aspects of the speech that may involve your interests. For example, do you have a relationship (e.g., student–teacher relationship, workplace relationship, friendship, etc.) with the speaker or with other members of the audience? Consider what impact your nonverbal cues will have on the relationship you have with the speaker and with other audience members.

- **Close-mindedness.** When receivers are close-minded, they are intolerant of the views of others. For those believing that their views are superior to others, listening makes little sense. Effective listeners develop the capacity to be open to considering new ideas.

- **Not concentrating.** Receivers who give in to distractions develop poor listening habits. Develop the capacity to focus on the six listener responsibilities discussed in this section for ways to sharpen your concentration.

- **Listening too hard.** This occurs when we listen for every single detail of a speech instead of trying to grasp the "big picture" of what the main points of the speech are. Rather than listening to each detail, listen for the six listener responsibility factors discussed earlier in this section.

- **Jumping to conclusions.** Reserve judgments about the speech until it has been delivered. Effective listening requires the receiver to weigh all of the speaker's message rather than a limited and incomplete snapshot of the speech.

- **Focusing on delivery and personal appearance.** You will learn later in the semester how to evaluate a speaker on his or her delivery and personal appearance. What becomes problematic is when audience members focus only on delivery and appearance instead of the message itself.

Summary

Public speaking is a regular part of our lives. Although people have engaged in public speaking for thousands of years, preparing and delivering an effective speech remains a puzzle for many people. Following the successful completion of this course, you will deliver more effective speeches and have a greater understanding of how to evaluate the speeches of others.

Effective public speakers know how to prepare and deliver an impactful speech. An effective public speaker is guided by ethical standards in the preparation and delivery of a speech. Public speaking builds on the communication skills we acquired when we learned how to speak with others in interpersonal and group contexts. The public context expands that opportunity for interaction and, if carried out effectively, preserves the naturalness and spontaneity that we associate with good conversation.

Key Terms/Concepts to Know

Consumer of messages	Citing sources
Producer of messages	Listening
Ethics	Types of listening
Social responsibility	Effective listening
Individual responsibility	Filters
Plagiarism	

Grow Your Skill Sets

You may be familiar with the webpage *Ted: Ideas Worth Spreading*. This site is devoted to speeches involving a wide range of topics. The site can be found at http://www.ted.com/. Select a speech and:

- Listen for how the speaker cites his or her sources. How did you assess speakers who did not cite sources?

- Consider whether the speaker engaged in ethical speaking. What was the basis for your decision?

- Consider what type of listening you used. What kinds of filters impacted you during the speech?

Online Speech Resources

TED: Ideas Worth Spreading
http://www.ted.com/

TED is a nonprofit devoted to spreading ideas, usually in the form of short, powerful talks (18 minutes or less). TED began in 1984 as a conference where Technology, Entertainment and Design converged, and today covers almost all topics—from science to business to global issues—in more than 100 languages. Meanwhile, independently run TEDx events help share ideas in communities around the world.

The Miller Center
http://millercenter.org/

The Miller Center is a nonpartisan affiliate of the University of Virginia that specializes in presidential scholarship, public policy, and political history. With the cooperation of various presidential libraries, the Miller Center has been collecting some of the most important presidential speeches in American history. These speeches all have transcripts, and some are available in their entirety in audio or video.

The History Channel
http://www.history.com/speeches

The Famous Speeches & Audio page of the History Channel includes several hundred audio and video speeches from speakers over the past 90 years.

Iowa State University Archives
of Women's Political Communication
http://www.womenspeecharchive.org/links/

Women are being elected to public office in increasing numbers. However, their voices remain largely underrepresented in collections and archives of political communication. For this reason, the Carrie Chapman Catt Center for Women and Politics at Iowa State University has created an online archive devoted entirely to women's political speeches.

Vital Speeches of the Day
http://vsotd.com/

Vital Speeches of the Day is a monthly collection of the best speeches in the world.

Reference List

Brownell, J. (2013). *Listening: Attitudes, principles, and skills* (5th ed.). Boston, MA: Pearson/Allyn & Bacon.

Dean of Students. (2005). *Hilltopics: Student handbook*, 2006–2007. Knoxville, University of Tennessee.

Farmer, P. (2013). On empathy and reasoning. Retrieved May 16, 2014 from http://www.udel.edu/udaily/2013/may/address052613.html.

Floyd, J.J. (1985). *Listening: A practical approach*. Glenview, IL: Scott-Foresman.

Fox, M.V. (1983). Ancient Egyptian rhetoric. *Rhetorica*, 1, 9–22.

Gallo, C. (2012). 11 presentation lessons you can still learn from Steve Jobs. Retrieved November 1, 2012 from http://www.forbes.com/sites/carminegallo/2012/10/04/11-presentation-lessons-you-can-still-learn-from-steve-jobs/.

Harnden, T. (2012). Time to get a new speechwriter, minister? Aussie politician rips off line from Michael Douglas film The American President. Retrieved January 27, 2012 from http://www.daily-mail.co.uk/news/article-2091710/Tony-Abbott-attack-Anthony-Albanese-rips-line-Michael-Douglas-film-The-American-President.html.

Josephson Institute Quotations: Respect. Retrieved January 29, 2014 from http://josephsoninstitute.org/quotes/quotations.php?q=Respect.

Murphy, J.J., Katula, R.A., & Hoppmann, M. (2014). *A synoptic history of classical rhetoric* (4th ed.). New York: Routledge.

National Communication Association (1999). *NCA Credo for Ethical Communication*. Retrieved December 30, 2013 from http://www.natcom.org/uploadedFiles/About_NCA/Leadership_and_Governance/Public_Policy_Platform/PDF-PolicyPlatform-NCA_Credo_for_Ethical_Communication.pdf.

Nilsen, T. R. (1974). *Ethics of speech communication* (2nd ed.). Indianapolis: Bobbs-Merrill.

Pearson, J.C., Child, J.T., Mattern, J.L., & Kahl, D.H. (2006). What are students being taught about ethics in public speaking classes? *Communication Quarterly*, 54, 507–521.

PLAGIARISM EXERCISE

You will be gathering information as you prepare for each speech assignment. Use this exercise to determine whether you can recognize plagiarism. Read the following selection and decide whether the passage requires a citation and if the citation is used accurately and appropriately. What, if anything, would you do to improve the passages below?

From the article:

INTERNET CRIME: CYBER CRIME—A NEW BREED OF CRIMINAL?
Kit Burden and Creole Palmer

Computer Law and Security Review

Volume 19, Issue 3, May 2003, Pages 222–227

The "cyber criminal" sounds like a term to be applied to someone from a William Gibson book, and yet is all too real, and on a day to day basis wreaks havoc in our increasingly online world. In April 2001, the Government responded to this threat by announcing a $25 million initiative involving the creation of a National High-Tech Crime Unit to counter the growing use of the Internet for criminal activity. The online world is becoming increasingly vulnerable to criminal activity with 43% of the public identifying cybercrime as a 'problem'.

Speaker One
According to Burden and Palmer in an article published in _Computer Law and Security Review_, less than 50% of the public believes cybercrime is a problem.

Speaker Two
Internet crime is one type of crime that takes place in the U.S.

Speaker Three
The National High-Tech Crime Unit was created in 2001 to counter growing cybercrime activity as reported by Burden and Palmer in a 2003 article published in the journal _Computer Law and Security Review_.

CHAPTER 2

A BRIEF HISTORY OF PUBLIC SPEAKING

CHAPTER OBJECTIVES

This chapter is designed to help you understand:

- The history of public speaking

- The importance of both speech delivery and speech content

- The role of different cultures across time in public speaking

- Contemporary public speaking

Georgios Kollidas / Shutterstock.com

Public speaking has been part of the fabric of human society for more than 5,000 years. While many of our ideas about public speaking span that time frame, modern communication technologies present speakers with new opportunities as well as new challenges when sharing their ideas with receivers. The task confronting speakers in this age of ever-changing communication technologies is to integrate new ways of conveying information with time-tested understandings of effective public speaking.

No one knows exactly when humans began to engage in public speaking. It is clear, however, that ancient peoples from different regions and different cultures valued public speaking. For example, the Maori peoples of New Zealand, the ancient Egyptians, the ancient Chinese, and ancient Aztecs as well as the ancient Greeks all developed rich and varied public speaking traditions. The tradition of study and instruction that has been most influential to speakers in the U.S. can be traced to the ancient Greeks and Romans. This tradition of study and instruction flourished in Medieval Europe and eventually came to take the form of 21st-century public speaking. From its beginnings, two themes were associated with our ancestor's interest in public speaking. First, it was recognized that skillful, eloquent speakers were prized by members of society. Thus, most all ancient traditions placed a high value on the delivery of a speech. Second, it was recognized that speakers should conform to a set of organizational and ethical guidelines when engaging in public speaking. Thus, the content of a speech was also recognized as key to effective public speaking. To begin our discussion of the history of public speaking, we will first consider two key concepts around which public speaking has been studied.

Delivery vs. Content

Study and instruction in public speaking has been characterized by a range of viewpoints about the importance of different parts of the speech process. In particular, the views of our ancestors varied considerably on the importance that should be assigned to the **content** of the message and the importance assigned to the delivery of a message. As illustrated in the textbox to the left, the debate continues today.

When you learn how to evaluate a speech/speaker effectively, you will most likely place more emphasis on the speaker's delivery and less on speech organization, citations, relevance, and other content components. The more messages you evaluate the more you will realize the importance of the content regardless of the skill with which the speech is delivered. As mentioned in Chapter One, a listener should seek to understand and analyze the speech in terms of the criteria for effective listening. The speech could be well organized with very relevant and useful information, but be delivered by a less than satisfactory speaker (good speech/poor speaker). Would this keep you from listening to the message?

On the other hand, you may encounter a speaker who is very conversational, enthusiastic, and passionate, but is delivering a poorly organized speech with confusing explanations that both keep you from fully understanding the message and/or recognizing unethical content. Would the speaker's delivery keep you from realizing this? Consider Adolf Hitler. He is known as one of the most persuasive speakers in history. He convinced his supporters to believe in his viewpoint and carry out horrible crimes against millions of people. Were they so taken by this man's delivery that they were willing to overlook the truth or rightness of his message? Many people are scammed or deceived every day by messages on television, the Internet, and from others in their life because they cannot properly evaluate both the content and delivery effectively. A speaker's content and delivery work together in a speech. Inexperienced evaluators often have difficulty because it is not easy to train the ear to listen to different aspects of content and delivery at once. Remember, you are not only evaluating the content that is conveyed by the speaker but the content that should be included. The more often you evaluate speeches, the better you will become at making sense of the way content and delivery work together.

A CASE IN POINT: DELIVERY VS. CONTENT

The School of Communication Studies sponsors a public speaking contest each semester that is open to all students enrolled in the public speaking course. After one contest a friendly dispute arose between some of the student members of the audience and the judges. One student who delivered a very dynamic, skillful speech finished third in the competition. Based on his skillful delivery, the students argued that this speaker should have won the contest. However, the judges expressed reservations about the content of the speech. Specifically, the speaker did not cite sources. As one judge explained, "Delivery by itself cannot substitute for a sound message. An effective speaker delivers a well-reasoned message that is supported by a variety of sources and is well organized."

What do you think? Does delivery trump content?

Historical Overview

Public speaking traditions are as old as human civilization. In fact, two thousand years **before** public speaking was studied among the ancient Greeks, the Mesopotamians evolved the first public speaking tradition of civilized man (Willis, 1970). This early public speaking tradition can be traced to approximately 2,700 B.C. The evidence from this ancient time suggests that speakers engaged in many of the same behaviors that speakers engage in today. For example, a speaker was expected to rise and deliver the speech while standing. Speakers used their voice and hand gestures for dramatic effect. Interestingly, there are recorded instances in which speakers used visual aids (a bow used in war in one instance and jewelry in a second instance). While we credit the ancient Mesopotamians with the development of public speaking, it was perhaps the ancient Egyptians who began to study public speaking in systematic fashion.

THE EGYPTIANS

One of the earliest references to public speaking comes from a work generally regarded as one of the oldest books in the world (Rawnsley, 1912; Wilson, 1951). The document entitled *The Precepts of Ptah-Hotep* dates to approximately 2,200 B.C. and is characteristic of what has come to be known as the Egyptian wisdom literature. This type of manuscript was written by a father to his son as well as other pupils, sharing the wisdom of the ages, as well as offering advice on how a person should conduct himself in public and private matters. The father or teacher promised that conformity to these teachings would result in divine favor and professional success (Fox, 1983).

Throughout this 4,200-year-old manuscript Ptah-Hotep stressed the importance of public speaking. Ptah-Hotep viewed "rhetoric" as the principles that guide fine speech. An eloquent speaker was valued as a rare jewel. While it might appear that Ptah-Hotep and his contemporaries valued delivery above content, he cautioned that learning was essential *prior* to taking on the role of a public speaker. Those who would become effective speakers learned first to listen and master the principles of fine speech.

Effective public speaking in ancient Egypt conformed to five major canons or rules. First, effective speakers did not boast. Second, say no more than what is needed. Third, do not bully or demean those of lower rank when speaking with them. Fourth, a speaker who is under control (i.e., not yelling, boasting, or emotional) will be viewed as more competent and knowledgeable. Fifth, speak when your ideas are well formed rather than engaging in speaking with no preparation (Fox, 1983).

As discussed, early interest in public speaking study and instruction was not limited to ancient Egypt. Peoples in other parts of the world such as China, India, Africa, and New Zealand also placed a high value on public address. However, the public speaking traditions that sprang from ancient Greece have been most influential on our practice of public speaking.

Make thyself a craftsman in speech, for thereby thou shalt gain the upper hand.

—Inscription found in a 3,000-year-old Egyptian tomb

Aristotle 384–322 B.C.

ARE YOU FAMILIAR WITH THE SPEECH SUPER HEROES?

The "Fantastic Four" ancient Greek philosophers that continue to influence our thinking on effective speaking include Aspasia, Socrates, Plato, and Aristotle.

THE GREEKS

The influence of the ancient Greeks on public speaking began in the Greek city-state of Syracuse located on the island of Sicily in the early fifth century B.C.E. Many scholars attribute to Corax and his pupil Tisias the first systematic formulation of principles for effective public speaking (Conley, 1990; McCroskey, 1997). Corax developed an interest in public speaking because of the events that he witnessed going on around him. Syracuse was governed by a tyrant named Gelon who had seized all property and land. In 465 B.C. the citizens of Syracuse overthrew this dictator and made it possible for people to pursue claims in court for the return of their property. However, the new government did not allow citizens to use lawyers to plead their case. Citizens were required to represent themselves in court and explain why they should be awarded the property. Not surprisingly, Corax observed that many people lost court cases because they were unable to communicate effectively in court settings. Therefore, he established a school to teach public speaking skills to former landowners. The public speaking practices he developed and recorded for court presentations he called ***rhetoric***, or the science of persuasion.

That system of public speaking guidelines was more fully developed by a number of ancient Greeks that included scholars such as Aristotle, Protagoras, Gorgias, Isocrates, and Plato. These scholars did not agree on exactly what should be studied or taught in public speaking but they shared the belief that effective public speaking skills were essential for success in life. Taken together, the work of the Greek scholars brought structure and coherence to study and instruction in public speaking. They recognized that the speech making process could be broken down into its component parts for systematic study in order to better understand how each part worked.

Perhaps the most influential of this group of scholars was Aristotle. It is commonly believed that his work entitled *Rhetoric* is the single most influential document ever composed on public address (Conley, 1990; McCroskey, 1997). **Aristotle's *Rhetoric*** consists of series of books that divide study and instruction in public speaking into three major divisions: the speaker, the audience, and the message. Aristotle's first book in this series focuses on invention or the development of lines of argument by the speaker. In addition, this work also distinguishes among different kinds of speaking settings (such as to a legislature or court of law) that would result in the need for the development of different lines of argument. The second book focuses on the nature of the audience and the kinds of emotions the speech might elicit in the listeners. Aristotle recognized that listeners might respond differently to a message based on factors such as their age, education, or financial state. The third book concerns questions of style. His view of delivery focused on speaker clarity and, to a lesser degree, politeness and liveliness.

While Aristotle's work continues to influence our views on the reasoning behind messages used by speakers, other Greek scholars such as Isocrates made significant contributions to study and instruction in speech delivery (Conley, 1990). Isocrates' view of public speaking rests on the belief that individuals will never achieve complete knowledge on any topic. Instead, individuals possess the ability to develop informed opinions leading to reasonable courses of action. These informed opinions and reasonable courses of action provide the basis for developing speeches. For Isocrates, speaking well was a sign that the speaker possessed a sound understanding of the topic being discussed. His view of effective public speaking included a very distinctive, ornate speaking style. The style he advocated would play an important role in the ancient Roman study and instruction of public speaking.

The ideas of the ancient Greeks continue to influence how we study and teach public speaking. In fact, many believe that today's scholars and teachers of public speaking have simply refined the ideas of the ancient Greeks.

THE ROMANS

The Greek tradition of instruction and study in public speaking began to appear in ancient Rome toward the end of the 2nd century B.C. Initially the Romans had reservations about the Greek view of public speaking but soon began to adopt the public speaking practices used by the Greeks (Conley, 1990). Consistent with the ancient Greeks, the Romans viewed public speaking skills as essential to success in public life. Many Roman scholars involved in study and instruction in public speaking sought to bring together several important social issues (education, philosophy, citizenship, and oratory) into a single worldview. This worldview is captured by the idea of a good man speaking well in his public and private life. Overall, the ancient Roman contribution to study and instruction in public speaking was to clarify and refine the work of the Greeks.

The Roman Forum

Perhaps the most influential Roman scholar of public address was Cicero. Cicero was greatly influenced by the ideas of the Greek scholar Isocrates and the importance of an eloquent speaking style. Moreover, since he did not believe speakers could ever attain perfect knowledge of a topic, he felt it was important for a speaker to be able to argue both sides of an issue. Cicero felt that the most effective public speaker would also be the best man, and use his speaking skills to persuade others to adopt the correct way to live. This view places public speaking at the center of society and how it functions. Oratory skills were highly valued and were considered the mark of an educated person. It was during this time that it came to be believed that a broad-based liberal arts education was essential to the development of a public speaker.

Confucius 551–479 B.C.

PUBLIC SPEAKING TRANSCENDS TIME AND CULTURE

"Injustice anywhere is a threat to justice everywhere."

—Martin Luther King, Jr., 1963

"Where there are fallacies or heresies in society, scholars can use public speaking to fight against it."

—Hsun Tzu, 310–220 B.C.

THE CHINESE

The Chinese developed a rich tradition of public speaking that was independent of the Greek and Roman traditions but shared much in common. Public speaking and argumentation as practiced in China from 500 B.C. emphasized the creation of logic, morality, and knowledge (Lu & Frank, 1993). In addition, the Chinese tradition also emphasized the role of public speaking in achieving social order and justice.

Confucius, a Chinese scholar, teacher, and politician, played a key role in developing the public speaking tradition in China, and his ideas continue to influence Chinese speakers to this day. From his view, a skillful orator should strive to bring about appropriate social order and social harmony. Later scholars such as Hsun Tzu extended the ideas of Confucius in somewhat different directions but continued to emphasize logic and morality.

THE EUROPEANS

From the third century until the Renaissance, the public speaking tradition inherited by European scholars from the ancient Greeks and Romans was carried on with little change. The burst of interest in public address during the Renaissance was accompanied by an increased importance placed on style and delivery. Well-known scholars such as Petrus Ramus viewed public speaking study and instruction as involving style and delivery. He assigned the reasoning associated with the development of messages to an area of study he labeled logic. Although some notable scholars such as Leonard Cox and Thomas Wilson continued to study and teach the reasoning and delivery components of public speaking, the dominant view of public speaking in the Renaissance separated these two major components of speaking (Campbell, 1996).

CONTEMPORARY PUBLIC SPEAKING

The tradition of public speaking inherited by the U.S. was influenced by the Greeks, Romans, and Europeans. Thus, the debates concerning the importance of the message and the importance of delivery in the public speaking process made their way to the United States. This debate led to the development of what has come to be known as the **elocutionary** movement. The goal of those who founded the group was to use a "new science" to study the laws that underlie human behavior in public speaking situations (Campbell, 1996). It was hoped that through systematic study we could arrive at a scientifically based knowledge of voice and body movement (delivery), so as to learn what kind of style is natural and, as a result, most effective. The critics of the elocutionary movement argued that the style adopted by the elocutionists was anything but natural. Although the elocutionists were highly influential in the study and teaching of public speaking during the late eighteenth and nineteenth centuries, they have little influence today.

The most important influence on public speaking in the twenty-first century has come from scholars guided by the social sciences. Changes in the way we gather, store, and retrieve information have impacted how speakers prepare and the ways they may share information with the audience. Speakers and receivers now have greater access to information, and speakers are able to present information in more ways than at any point in the past. Social scientific inquiry into persuasion and attitudes has impacted how we study and teach persuasive speaking. Moreover, the widespread use of information technology has changed how we communicate in public speaking situations. This has created new opportunities, as well as new challenges, for speakers.

The new opportunities that information technology has provided speakers cover a wide range of issues. First, speakers now have much greater access to information that aids in speech preparation. In fact, this course now includes a unit on the library and its services that is designed to assist you in learning about search engines, sources of information, and the quality of the information available through information technology. Second, speakers have a greater number of ways of presenting information to members of the audience as a result of advances in information technology. For example, you will have access to PowerPoint® presentation software, the Web, and audio/video equipment when delivering your presentations.

The challenges presented by information technology tend to involve its use or misuse. That is, people often use technology poorly (using only the first source of information generated by a Google search, developing a PowerPoint® slide show to substitute for you as a speaker, and so on). One goal of this course is to strengthen your understanding of the appropriate uses of information technology.

Advances in information technology have also offered us greater access to a wider variety of speaking traditions from across the globe. Not all peoples embrace the speaking tradition that can be traced to the Greeks and Romans. We encourage you to visit the School of Communication Studies webpage for more information concerning the speaking traditions of different cultures.

Summary

This brief overview was not meant to provide the reader with a comprehensive understanding of the history of public speaking over the past 4,500 years. Rather, it is our goal that you recognize that public speaking has a very long history. Peoples from different cultures in different locations across the planet at different points in time recognized that public speaking has an impact on the quality of a person's life. Many of our basic ideas about public speaking may be traced to the Greeks and Romans, but recall that the public speaking traditions of many peoples have contributed to our current understanding of how public speaking should take place. Those ideas will continue to be refined in this age of information and technological change. In the next section, we will begin to consider how public speaking fits into our understanding of the communication process.

STUDENT NOTES

Key Terms/Concepts to Know

Delivery	Roman tradition
Content	Chinese tradition
Egyptian tradition	European tradition
Greek tradition	Elocutionary movement

Publications and Online Speech Resources

Publications

Rhetoric Before and Beyond the Greeks—edited by Carol S. Lipson and Roberta A. Binkley (2004)

The African Origins of Rhetoric—by Cecil Blake (2009)

Rhetoric in Ancient China, Fifth to Third Century, B.C.E.: A Comparison with Classical Greek Rhetoric—by Xing Lu (1998)

Online Resources

The Rise of Rhetoric in Ancient Greece—YouTube https://www.youtube.com/watch?v=6egBSZN5Dkc

Public Speaking: The ACA Open Knowledge Online Guide—http://textcommons1.org/node/102

References

Campbell, K.K. (1996). *The Rhetorical Act*. Belmont: Wadsworth Publishing Company.

Conley, T.M. (1990). *Rhetoric in the European tradition*. Chicago: University of Chicago Press.

Fox, M.V. (1983). Ancient Egyptian rhetoric. *Rhetorica*, 1, 9–22.

Lu, Xing, & Frank, D.A. (1993). On the study of ancient Chinese rhetoric. *Western Journal of Communication*, 57, 445–463.

McCroskey, J.C. (1997). *An introduction to rhetorical communication* (7th ed.). Boston: Allyn & Bacon.

Rawnsley, H.D. (1912). *Notes for the Nile: Together with a metrical rendering of the hymns of ancient Egypt and of the precepts of Ptah-hotep (the oldest book in the world)*. Leipzig: F.A. Brocklaus.

Willis, J.W. (1970). Speaking arenas of ancient Mesopotamia. *Quarterly Journal of Speech*, 56, 398–405.

Wilson, J.A. (1951). The instructions of Vizier Ptah-Hotep. *Ancient Near Eastern Texts*, New York: Princeton University Press.

THE COMMUNICATION PROCESS

CHAPTER OBJECTIVES

This chapter is designed to help you understand:

- The communication process

- Models of communication

- Differences between communication models

- Communication contexts

- Communication and culture

- Intercultural communication

Most all of us engage in communication on a daily basis. We interact in a variety of different contexts that involve school, family, work, and recreation. And, on occasion, we interact in contexts that involve public speaking. Despite our frequent use of communication, people often have a very limited understanding of how communication works. If you are not sure what is meant by this, consider the following question:

What happens when communication occurs?

Most responses to that question are so general or vague ("I open my mouth and words come out.") as to be nearly useless in explaining what happens when people communicate. In this chapter, we will examine the communication process and consider how communication works. From its inception, those interested in public speaking have sought to better understand the factors that impact the way we communicate in public speaking contexts. A better understanding of

It is a craftsman who can speak in counsel, for speaking is more difficult than any labor.

—Ptah-Hotep,
The Precepts of Ptah-Hotep
(circa 2,200 B.C.)

what happens when communication occurs will help you to advance your speaking skills. We begin this discussion with an overview of the communication process and explore the way communication works in public speaking situations.

The Communication Process

The concept of communication means different things to different people. For some, communication involves messages in the mass media. For others, communication involves interaction between two or more people who seek to achieve a common understanding. For still others, communication involves the physiological processes necessary to produce verbal messages. Given the wide-ranging meanings people assign communication, it is not surprising that it is difficult to settle on a single definition of communication.

Although few terms have as many meanings as communication, there is general agreement that a definition of communication includes the following:

- Communication is a process;

- Communication involves the use of symbols; and

- Communication involves a sharing or exchanging of meanings.

While general agreement exists on some features of a communication definition, people disagree on other issues that help us to define communication. Perhaps the most important of these issues concerns intention. **Intention** has proven to be a difficult issue to resolve in definitions of communication. For some, communication need not be intentional. Indeed, many believe that one cannot, not communicate. The implication of this view is that all we do is considered communication. While many agree with this perspective, others find this view of communication too broad. For many, the intentional production of messages has a quality that separates it from other kinds of human behavior. Thinking about communication in this way suggests that individuals are pursuing a goal or set of goals through the intentional use of symbolic behavior when they communicate with others. The implication of this view is that our understanding of communication is limited to purposeful interaction.

In this course you will engage in a number of activities that involve purposeful interaction. That is, you will deliver speeches that will be designed to inform, persuade, and entertain, inspire, or introduce. Therefore, for the purpose of this course, we adopt a working **definition of communication** as the process of intentionally stimulating meaning in the mind of another.

Models of Communication

One way to develop a better understanding of a concept like communication is to construct a visual representation of what happens when communication takes place. A visual representation has the advantage of bringing into focus how different component parts such as a source and a receiver work together. As you will recall, the work of many ancient scholars such as Aristotle was directed toward dividing the public speaking process into component parts in order to better understand how it works.

Simply put, a model is a simplified version of the real thing. For example, a model car is a simplified version of a real car. It does not include all of the parts of the actual car, but it does provide a visual summary of the key parts: the wheels, the body, the engine, and so on. Since many different models could be developed to represent a single car, we should consider what counts as a "good" model. The way that we judge the worth of a model is to evaluate how well the model represents the real thing. In our model car example we would judge a model that includes wheels that move and a hood that can be raised as superior to a model with wheels that do not move and a hood that cannot be raised.

Models can also be helpful in diagnosing why communication is ineffective. Models tell us how the parts of communication work together. They make clear if one thing leads to another or if the parts are expected to work at the same time.

Although many different models of communication exist, for the purpose of this course we will focus on two models. The **Source Message Channel Receiver** (SMCR) model, also known as the linear model, is one of the oldest and simplest models of communication. It was developed by David Berlo, a scholar and administrator at Michigan State University. It is sometimes called the linear model because it suggests that communication works in linear or straight line-like fashion. The model suggests that when communication takes place, several things occur in a specific order and that communication is only moving in one direction. The model is presented below and includes the factors that are associated with each source, message, channel, and receiver category:

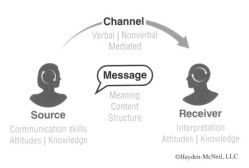

©Hayden-McNeil, LLC

Source Message Channel Receiver Model of Communication

The speaker is considered the **source**. The speaker encodes a **message** that is considered the content of what he/she is attempting to communicate. The **channel** is the particular way in which the message is communicated (e.g., sound, visual, smell, etc.) to the receiver. The **receiver**, or audience, decodes the message and makes an interpretation of what the speaker means. Each party in the communication has a single role as either a source or a receiver. This model has the advantage of being simple and easily understood, but it does have drawbacks. For example, the SMCR model does not include feedback. Feedback involves the nonverbal or verbal response from receivers that are sent back to a speaker in reaction to a message. In situations where there is little, if any, opportunity for feedback, the SMCR model can provide an adequate representation of what takes place during communication. However, if we encounter other situations where issues such as feedback are taking place during a speech, the SMCR model will not adequately represent what is taking place. In this case, we would need a different model to represent what is happening.

A second model of communication that is often used to help people understand what happens when communication occurs is called the **transactional model**.

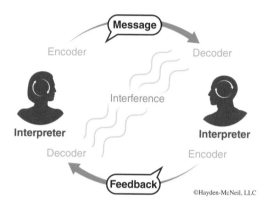

©Hayden-McNeil, LLC

Transactional Model

The transactional model offers a different way of representing what happens when we communicate. In this model, people send and receive messages simultaneously. During this simultaneous transaction, **interference** (any factor that inhibits the exchange of meaning or impedes the message) and **context** (the surrounding environment or situation) impact the encoding and decoding of messages. This model is more complex in that communicators are represented as doing more. That is, they construct and deliver messages at the same time that they receive and interpret messages. This model suggests that communication is a more complex activity than is represented in the SMCR model.

DIFFERENCES BETWEEN MODELS

The most important difference between the SMCR model and the transactional model involves the kinds of roles that people play when engaging in public speaking situations. In the SMCR model a person is either a sender or a receiver. In the transactional model, a person is both, allowing for feedback. As mentioned previously, **feedback** involves the nonverbal or verbal response from receivers that are sent back to a speaker in reaction to a message. In addition, the transactional model adds two new factors: context and interference. This model suggests that context and interference will influence what happens when we communicate. **Context** involves situational factors that influence how communicators interpret their surroundings. **Interference** may be thought of as factors that block or inhibit the receipt of a message by either receiver. Interference can be silent or make sound (noise) and come from within your audience or from outside of your audience. For example, if an audience member is giving in to mental distractions, it is interference since it's keeping them from receiving the message even though it is silent and comes from within the audience. Based on the transactional model, effective speakers make use of the context and seek to minimize interference in order to achieve objectives with listeners.

So, which model best describes what happens when we communicate in public speaking situations? The answer is that it depends on the setting for the public speaking event. For example, when a U.S. president delivers a speech from the Oval Office in the White House, the audience views the speech on television. In this situation the President does not receive feedback from the television audience during the speech, and occupies the role of sender. The people watching the speech on television occupy the receiver role. It is later that the roles are exchanged. The President takes on the role of receiver as responses to the speech begin to appear in the press or through polls. Audience members take on the role of sender as they respond to poll questions or provide feedback through the mass media.

In many cases, a speaker delivers the speech in front of an audience. In this situation the speaker sends messages while receiving messages from those in the audience. The nonverbal and verbal messages of the audience provide immediate feedback to the speaker. Thus, when delivering a speech in front of an audience, all parties in the event are senders and receivers. This setting allows the speaker an opportunity to respond to the messages that he/she is receiving, and adapt the speech to the audience.

Public Speaking vs. Other Communication Contexts

Based on our working definition, all communication may be defined as the process of intentionally stimulating meaning in the mind of another. However, we communicate in many different contexts such as interpersonal, group, and organizational settings. Each of these contexts differs in terms of the number of people engaging in communication (for example, interpersonal contexts involve two people; group contexts involve three to twelve people, and so on), the roles that people are expected to play, and a number of other factors. How does public speaking differ from other communication contexts?

Public speaking differs from other communication contexts in several ways. The differences include:

- **Planning/preparation**. The person delivering the speech must engage in much more planning and preparation for the event than normally occurs in other communication contexts. For example, we do not normally prepare and practice for the conversations we have with family or friends.

- **Degree of formality**. Speeches tend to be viewed as more formal occasions than our day-to-day conversations. Both verbal and nonverbal language are more formal in a public speech. For example, you would not use slang terms or slouch as much in a speech the way you would talking one-on-one with a friend.

- **Communication rules**. Many of the rules we use to guide conversation do not apply in public speaking situations. For example, we expect in conversation that people take turns making contributions to the discussion. In public speaking situations, this type of turn-taking would be considered inappropriate. For public speaking, an example of a communication rule would be to applaud after a speech. Try applauding your friend after he or she tells you about his or her weekend and see what reaction you receive.

Intercultural Communication: Delivering Messages in a Global Environment

Diversity is an increasingly prominent part of everyday life. Regardless of where people live in the United States, they encounter others with different nationalities, religions, cultural backgrounds, and belief systems. Consider the following statistical information. In the 1970s, roughly 12% of the population was black, Hispanic, or Asian-American. According to the 2010 U.S. census, approximately 28% of the U.S. population was composed people from these groups. One in four people in the U.S. practice a religion that falls outside of Christianity. Moreover, population trends suggested by the 2010 U.S. census indicate that Hispanics and Asian-Americans are the fastest growing groups in the country. In east Tennessee, Hispanics constitute the fastest growing segment of the population (U.S. Census, 2011).

You now live in an age when all of the people on earth, regardless of their background or culture, are interconnected. Some of these connections may be apparent during the course of your day-to-day life when someone with an unusual accent speaks to you or you interact with someone wearing clothing that you do not associate with "mainstream" culture. Other connections may have broader implications for life in the U.S. such as the effect the "Arab Spring" has had on American political thought or the influence of English musical artists on their U.S. counterparts. More than ever, it seems that what happens in one place touches all parts of the world. As a communicator, your success depends on how you adapt and relate to other members of this global communication environment.

INTERCULTURAL COMMUNICATION DEFINED

Our most significant values, beliefs, and attitudes are rooted in culture. Culture provides communicators with a lens through which they understand and interpret the world around them. While you may communicate most often with people who share your cultural understandings, you do encounter people in your classes or where you work who embrace a different cultural worldview. When communicating with someone you view as culturally different, you are experiencing intercultural communication. Intercultural communication may be defined as "interaction between two people whose cultural perceptions and symbol systems are distinct enough to alter the communication event" (Samovar, Porter, McDaniel, 2007, p. 10). The ways in which communication events are altered spring from the cultural differences that exist between people involved in the interaction.

The role of culture is the key to understanding our definition of intercultural communication. When thinking of culture, many people may think of groups that represent different national backgrounds. National cultures do exist, and they play an important role in shaping the way people communicate. However, there are many factors that define a culture and shape the way people communicate. These factors include:

- Race/ethnicity

- Nationality/geographic region

- Age

- Physical ability/disability

- Socioeconomic status

- Gender

- Language

- Religious affiliation

- Political affiliation

With these factors in mind, we will define culture as "a learned set of shared interpretations about beliefs, values, and norms which affect the behaviors of a relatively large group of people" (Lustig & Koester, 2003, p. 27).

It is important to understand that culture is learned—it is not innate. By this we mean culture is not a quality that people possess at birth. For example, there is no preexisting cultural identity for Koreans or Jordanians or Canadians. People begin to acquire knowledge of the culture they were born into soon after birth. When a person achieves competence in a particular culture, he or she has become enculturated. As a result of being born into U.S. culture, you began at an early age to think and act differently than people born in Poland or Nigeria or New Zealand. Interestingly, these ways of thinking and acting tend to be taken for granted. Cultures are invisible to the people used to inhabiting them. But for people from different cultures, it is obvious that culture exerts enormous influence in how people live and communicate with one another.

One final consideration we wish you to consider about culture. Simply put, we cannot say that one culture is superior to all other cultures. As communicators, we can (and should!) recognize that other cultures exist and adapt our messages accordingly. However, operating from the view that "my" culture is superior to others is often the root cause of conflict between peoples embracing different cultural perspectives.

CHAPTER 3

Too often a superficial knowledge of other cultures tends to breed negative judgments when cultural differences come into view. The kind of negative evaluation that is sometimes assigned to a different culture is illustrated well by a quote from the ancient Greek playwright Aeschylus who wrote over two thousand years ago, "Everyone is quick to blame the alien" (Kerrigan, 1998).

The experience of intercultural communication can be uncomfortable for some. Understanding and appreciating cultural differences, separating important cultural differences from those that are inconsequential, and interpreting messages as intended by the sender present very real challenges to effective communication. One useful practice to follow when seeking to understand people from different cultures is to learn about their proverbs. Proverbs communicate the widespread beliefs and values of people from a particular culture. For example, in the U.S. it is common to say that "actions speak louder than words." Americans embrace a "doing" culture and getting things done is highly valued in the U.S. Interestingly, as the following concepts suggest, people across the globe share many ideas but may express them differently:

- **Sweep only in front of your own door.** This German proverb reflects the very private nature of the Germans and their strong dislike of gossip. There is a somewhat similar proverb found in Swedish culture: *He who stirs another's porridge often burns his own.*

- **A zebra does not despise its stripes.** From the Maasai of Africa, this saying expresses the value of accepting things as they are. There is a similar proverb found in the Mexican culture: *I dance to the tune that is played.*

- **A man's tongue is his sword.** With this saying Arabs are taught to value words and use them in a powerful and forceful manner.

- **Those who know do not speak and those who speak do not know.** This famous doctrine, in the *Analects* of Confucius, stressing silence over talk is very different from the advice given in the previous Arab proverb.

- **When spider webs unite they can tie up a lion.** The Ethiopian proverb teaches the importance of collectivism and group solidarity. In the Japanese culture the same idea is expressed with the following proverb: *A single arrow is easily broken, but not in a bunch.* For the Yoruba of Africa, the same lesson is taught with the proverb that notes: *A single hand cannot lift the calabash to the head.*

CULTURAL DIFFERENCES AND COMMUNICATION

Cultural differences impact how people deliver presentations as well as how they respond to presentations. Some differences are more impactful than others, and in the following section we will examine many of the features of culture that have the potential to influence the success of your presentations.

1. **Formality**. During the course of a presentation, the speaker seeks to establish a relationship with the members of the audience. People in the U.S. often seek to establish informal relationships with audience members. For example, first names are often used when referring to self or others as a way of indicating friendliness and inclusiveness. However, in other cultures (e.g., German culture) it is generally considered inappropriate to adopt an informal presentation style.

2. **Social customs.** Most all cultures have established traditions or customs for speaking events. To the members of the culture, customs provide guidelines for what is appropriate in a public speaking setting. Not surprisingly, those not enculturated into a particular culture may have difficulty determining what is happening. For example, at the conclusion of a speech delivered in Ulm, Germany, the speaker from the U.S. was surprised by the reaction of the audience. Audience members did not clap at the conclusion of the speech. Rather, they lightly struck the tables they were seated at for approximately two minutes. According to custom, applause in Germany takes the form of lightly striking a table or other solid object rather than clapping hands.

3. **Dress.** Professional or business attire is the norm for speakers outside the U.S. Wearing the latest fashion or the traditional college uniform (i.e., jeans and t-shirts) as is often the case in the U.S. would be viewed as inappropriate in most cultures across the globe.

4. **Gender.** Conceptions of gender-related appropriateness in public speaking or presentation contexts vary considerably across cultures. In many cultures, women are restricted in terms of how they may participate as a speaker or as a member of the audience. Such restrictions are not limited to different cultures outside the U.S. Within the U.S., some cultural groups do place restrictions on when women may speak or how they may participate as members of the audience.

5. **Time.** In general, time is viewed in one of two ways across cultures. First, in many cultures (such as here in the U.S.) time is viewed in monochromic terms. That is, time is seen as something that is almost tangible—it is something that can be scheduled and tasks are arranged for designated times. Language use in the U.S. also reflects this view. In this culture we do not like to waste time, and we set aside time for others. Second, a polychromic view of time places more importance on relationships in communication events than on the role of time. In cultures such as Greece or Mexico, you establish or renew relationships before engaging in presentation events. Thus, in some cultures speaking on time and not going over the assigned time is essential; in other cultures maintaining the speaking schedule is subordinate to relational factors.

CHAPTER 3

The kinds of differences described can present challenges when you are preparing and delivering presentations. The table below summarizes how cultural characteristics influence public speaking and presentations in three separate cultures.

Table 3.1 Cultural Characteristics and Public Speaking/Presentations

	U.S.	JAPAN	MEXICO
Social unit	Individual	Group	Family
Authority relationships	Egalitarian	Hierarchical	Hierarchical
Basis for authority	Competence	Seniority	Trust
Attitude toward competition	Seeks	Avoids	Avoids
Importance of relationships	Helpful	Essential	Essential
Basis for status	Money/ competence	Title/position	Title/position
Role of formality	Medium	High	High
Sense of history	Low	High	High
Importance of time	High	High	Low

CONNECTING WITH DIVERSE AUDIENCES

Speakers can encounter a wide range of difficulties when dealing with a diverse audience, but these challenges can be dealt with if you follow a few common sense guidelines. According to Morreale (2010) there are three practices you can follow to avoid problems speaking with interculturally diverse audiences.

First, stay up-to-date with current events and trends. What is meant by Arab Spring? How are social movements being influenced by social networking websites? How is immigration discussed in the Presidential campaign? When a speaker uses terms that are out of date or uses inappropriately terms that have recently gained wide public circulation, the audience will rightly assume the speaker is out of touch.

Second, don't add irrelevant identifiers and/or associations. Avoid making statements that include identifiers such as the female officer or the male nurse or the Arab American scientist. Does it matter that the nurse is a male? Would it matter if the nurse was French? In most all cases, the answer is no. These kinds of identifiers are often worse than useless; they have the potential to focus audience attention on irrelevant qualities. Audience members may also wonder if the use of the identifiers and associations is strategic. That is, they may suspect that you were using identifiers for some purpose other than the surface level goal.

Third, avoid using stereotypical information in speeches. Even well intentioned people can make use of stereotypes that produce negative perceptions in audience members. Whether it's conveying the idea that all Southerners like country music or that student-athletes are not concerned about their grades, the problem is generalizing limited and inaccurate perceptions of a few people to all members of the group or race or gender.

INTERNATIONAL/INTERCULTURAL ONLINE RESOURCES

Scholarly Resources
International Communication Association
http://www.icahdq.org/

International Communication Gazette
http://gaz.sagepub.com/

International Journal of Communication
http://ijoc.org/ojs/index.php/ijoc

International Association for Media and Communication Research
http://iamcr.org/

Fact Books
CIA World Factbook
https://www.cia.gov/library/publications/the-world-factbook/

Internet Library for Librarians
http://www.itcompany.com/inforetriever/almanac.htm

Presentation Resources
Gifts of Speeches
http://gos.sbc.edu/

Great Speeches of the 20th Century
http://www.guardian.co.uk/theguardian/series/greatspeeches

UN Women
http://www.unwomen.org/category/speeches/

Speeches of Tony Blair
http://www.tonyblairoffice.org/speeches/

TED—Ideas Worth Spreading
http://www.ted.com/

TED—100 Websites to Know and Use
http://blog.ted.com/2007/08/03/100_websites_yo/

The world in which we speak has become increasingly diverse. You will be living and working with people who embrace different religions, values, experiences, and worldviews. Effective speakers recognize that there are different vantage points from which receivers understand their world. Factors such as age, gender, education, race, and ethnicity will have an impact on the values and beliefs embraced by receivers. Culturally insensitive speakers communicate clearly that their vantage point is THE vantage point from which to understand the world.

You can develop a number of strategies to overcome the barriers associated with a diverse audience. Consider the following:

- **Analyze your audience**. Learn about the cultural similarities and differences in your audience so that you can adapt your message to their vantage points. Later in the text you will be introduced to the process of audience analysis in preparation for a speech as well as when delivering a speech.

- **Reverse the roles**. Would you feel comfortable with a speaker from a different culture if he/she treats your cultural beliefs and values the way you plan to treat their cultural values and beliefs?

- **Avoid ethnocentrism**. **Ethnocentrism** may be defined as the belief that your worldview is superior to all others. Ethnocentric speakers are offensive to members of the audience who do not share that particular worldview. Unlike egocentrism, ethnocentrism is a group-related bias.

- **Learn the jargon.** Symbols (e.g., words or phrases, gestures, and so on) are not interpreted the same way across cultures. In fact, what may be viewed in one culture as a very positive symbol may have very negative connotations in a different culture. For example, the hand gesture referred to as the V or victory sign has very positive connotations in the U.S. but is interpreted as a very offensive gesture in many South American cultures.

The Speech Making Process

The speech making process itself involves a number of steps that you will use to prepare informative and persuasive speeches. As you begin the process of preparing, keep in mind the following:

- Always complete the body of the speech before the introduction and conclusion. The body of the speech determines what should be done with the introduction and the conclusion.

- Prepare visual aids after the speech has been written. The body of the speech determines what kind(s) of visual aid(s) should be used. Avoid the trap of creating visual aids first and deciding later how to develop the body of the speech.

- Audience analysis plays a role in every part of the speech—from preparation to delivery.

Key Terms/Concepts to Know

Communication definition

Intention

Models of communication

　　Source Message Channel Receiver model

　　Transactional model

　　Interference

　　Context

　　Feedback

Public speaking vs. other contexts

Intercultural communication definition

Cultural differences and communication

　　Formality

　　Social customs

　　Dress

　　Gender

　　Time

Connecting with diverse audiences

References

Kerrigan, J. (1998). *Revenge tragedy: Aeschylus to Armageddon*. New York: Oxford University Press.

Lustig, M.W., & Koester, J. (2003). *Intercultural competence: Interpersonal communication across cultures*, 4th ed. Boston: Allyn & Bacon.

Morreale, S.P. (2010). *The Competent Public Speaker*. New York: Peter Lang, Inc.

Samovar, L.A., Porter, R.E., & McDaniel, E.R. (2007). *Communication between Cultures*. New York: Thompson/Wadsworth.

U.S. Census (2011). United States Census 2010: It's in your hands. Retrieved from http://2010.census.gov/2010census/

CHAPTER 3

STUDENT NOTES

COMMUNICATION APPREHENSION

CHAPTER OBJECTIVES

This chapter is designed to help you understand:

- Speech anxiety

- The causes of speech anxiety

- Methods of managing speech anxiety

- How to manage speech anxiety when preparing and delivering a speech

- Developing confidence and credibility

Photo provided by John William Haas

Public speaking is often associated with communication apprehension. **Communication apprehension** may be thought of as the anxiety people experience when they think about or engage in communication. People experience communication apprehension in a variety of contexts or situations, such as interpersonal contexts, group contexts, and public speaking contexts. The anxiety that we experience when we think about or engage in public speaking is referred to as **speech anxiety**.

Speech anxiety is a common event. In fact, for many people in the United States, public speaking has been found to be their single greatest fear (even greater than death!). The anxiety that people experience may be expressed in a number of ways such as sweaty palms, shaking, rapid breathing, and so on. For many people, the anxiety they feel is very pronounced, and the symptoms of anxiety are more readily observable. For others, public speaking brings about a modest level of anxiety.

THOUGHTS ABOUT DEALING WITH SPEECH ANXIETY

You don't have to control your thoughts. You just have to stop letting them control you.

—Dan Millman

The best way to conquer stage fright is to know what you're talking about.

—Michael H. Mescan

Grasp the subject, the words will follow.

—Cato the Elder

I was pleasantly surprised to learn that people are actually interested in what I have to say.

—Anonymous student

Keep this thought in mind: A moderate level of anxiety is desirable when engaging in public speaking. The anxiety that is experienced when delivering a speech is a body's way of preparing you to perform well. The physiological changes that place us in this heightened state tend to make the individual more alert and physically prepared to perform. Regrettably, our body can go too far in preparing us to perform well. When this occurs, the speaker is experiencing a level of apprehension that can negatively impact on his/her performance.

Interestingly, there appear to be different kinds of speech anxiety. We can think about speech anxiety as a **trait** or as a **state**. Traits may be thought of as long-term, enduring characteristics that individuals possess. For example, adaptiveness is considered to be a trait that is important to skillful communication. The extent to which a person is able to adapt to changing circumstances tends to be fairly consistent. Thus, the trait view suggests that the level of speech anxiety a person experiences reflects a long-term, enduring quality of that individual when engaging in public speaking. The state view of speech anxiety suggests that anxiousness is brought about by particular situations. From this view a person may feel comfortable talking with peers prior to a speech. However, once the person begins to participate in public speaking, he or she will begin to experience some measure of apprehension. The following are major causes for state speech anxiety.

Causes for Speech Anxiety

There are many reasons why we may feel anxiety when delivering a speech. Below are the most common causes. Can you think of any others?

NUMBER OF AUDIENCE MEMBERS

For some, the more people that are added to their audience, the more nervous they become. For example, you may be less nervous speaking in front of a small class of twenty students and more nervous in front of a large lecture class of one hundred and twenty. Why do you think this occurs?

SPEAKER'S FAMILIARITY WITH AUDIENCE MEMBERS

How well you know the audience members has a large impact on the level of anxiety for speakers. Some feel more comfortable in front of an audience filled with strangers, while others are less nervous when they speak to individuals they know very well. The good news is that, in this course, your classmates will provide a balance between an audience that you will get to know as acquaintances but not to the extent of your close friends and family who know a lot about you. Which type of audience do you prefer?

FORMALITY OF THE SETTING

Regardless of who is in the audience, the location of a speech can affect the level of nervousness you experience when speaking. For example, most speakers would be more nervous on a stage, in an auditorium, and under a spotlight than they would be in a small classroom setting. In addition, using a podium sometimes lessens anxiety for speakers who are intimidated by standing in front of the audience without a barrier.

PAST EXPERIENCES OF THE SPEAKER

While having a number of positive speaking experiences allows you to build skills and aids in decreasing anxiety, a negative speaking experience in your past can cause your level of apprehension to be higher than average. You may have delivered a speech in seventh grade in front of your class and had a really bad experience. For every speaking event after, you may have experienced negative thoughts and a high level of anxiety even thinking about speaking in public. Many times, high anxiety could exist because of a lack of experience. If you do not remember ever speaking in front of an audience, you may not know what to expect, which leads us to the next cause.

SPEAKER'S FEAR OF FAILURE

This cause for anxiety is mainly from a lack of self-confidence. Sometimes it is an irrational thought or because of a negative past experience, as mentioned above. For many, the fear comes from being judged by others negatively or the pressure of speaking for a grade in class.

Since we know that there are a number of factors that contribute to a speaker's level of anxiety, we need to look at what occurs to and in people when they experience anxiety while speaking. There are a variety of things that occur, both physiological and mental. Some of these are visible to the audience, while others are not. These can range from sweating, turning red, stuttering, mind going blank, shaking, fidgeting, swaying, speaking fast, lack of eye contact, etc. What happens to you when you speak?

The reason that many of these occur is our body's response to the anxiety in the form of adrenaline. For many people, public speaking evokes a fight-or-flight response. Our mind sends a message to our body that we are in an emergency situation and the body responds with surges of adrenaline. The next section will discuss how to use this necessary response to propel you through your speech.

CHAPTER 4

Problem Thought Patterns—Change Your Thinking

Below you will find problematic thought patterns and ideas for changing these patterns.

DEFINITION	EXAMPLE	THOUGHT PATTERN TO CHANGE	THOUGHT PATTERN YOU SHOULD ADOPT
All or Nothing Thinking	When things are viewed in black and white terms	"My presentation wasn't what I hoped for; I failed completely."	No "perfect" presentation exists. Instead, concentrate on what you did well. Avoid criticizing yourself too harshly.
Over-generalization	When a single negative event is seen as a permanent pattern of failure	After giving one speech that was not successful, you are convinced that future speeches will be failures.	That speech is behind me; future speeches will be successful.
Jumping to Conclusions	When you draw negative conclusions about an event before you have the facts	You are convinced that you failed the speech, although you ended up getting a B−.	Take a "wait and see" approach before assuming the worst.
Fortune Telling	The tendency to anticipate that things will turn out badly, no matter how much practice or rehearsal is done	You decide before the speech that you will "bomb" the assignment, despite the fact that you are well prepared.	Preparation and practice

Methods to Manage Anxiety

The good news is that you can learn to manage speech anxiety. The methods that have been developed to manage speech anxiety are based on different ways of attacking the causes of the anxiety. These methods involve visualization, competence, and physiology.

VISUALIZATION

For many, a lack of self-confidence is a problem that leads to a higher level speech anxiety. The goal is to change how the individual perceives himself/herself when engaging in public speaking. For example, a technique known as visualization is often used to help a person "visualize" a successful speaking experience. Visualization is a technique that has been used successfully in the arts, business, and sports. Studies of the brain have revealed that **thoughts** produce the same kinds of mental instructions as **actions**. In effect, the idea here is that there is a mind-body connection. Thus, when a person preparing for a speech begins to visualize the event (many of the cognitive processes in the brain involving planning and motor control) they begin to train for the actual performance.

Visualization as a method of managing nervousness involves the speaker "placing" himself/herself in a hypothetical public speaking situation. Visualization is an activity that must take place prior to the speech. The goal of this method is to vividly imagine delivering a very effective speech. Simply put, you imagine yourself performing at a high level in a situation that causes nervousness (in this case, public speaking). Athletes participate in this method in order to perform better on the court, field, and so on. Repeatedly visualizing positive performance does appear to reduce fears of public speaking, because the positive image begins to replace the negative images involved with public speaking. Keep in mind that repeatedly visualizing a negative experience may lead to poor performance. Therefore, it is essential to visualize upcoming speaking experiences in a positive fashion.

Maintain a mental picture of you speaking well and achieving your speech objectives. Return to this mental image often and expect the best!

COMPETENCE

The goal is to reduce apprehension by strengthening the skills of the speaker so that he/she will become more competent at public speaking. If anxiety is brought about because the individual does not feel that he/she "knows how to" engage in public speaking, training designed to bring about effective public speaking skills will enable the speaker to manage speech anxiety.

- **Skills Training**. By enrolling in this course, you are engaging in skills training. As a method of managing nervousness, training requires the individual to gain additional experience as a speaker. People often experience nervousness because they perceive that they do not possess the skills necessary to perform well. You will begin to experience decreasing levels of nervousness as you build your speaking skills over the course of the semester.

PHYSIOLOGY

The goal is to address the symptoms (increased heart rate, nervous stomach, and so on) of communication apprehension so as to more effectively manage it. This approach involves techniques such as relaxation training, which includes taking deep breaths before your speech.

In the following section, we offer additional tips to manage your nervousness prior to the speech, as well as during the presentation.

CHAPTER 4

Before You Speak

- Think positively!

- Use visualization

- Do not expect perfection. Expect that you will communicate well despite any occasional mistake

- To bring about psychological relaxation before moving to the podium, imagine speaking to one person at a time. Determine to talk to the audience, not at them.

- Determine to communicate, not perform

- Get a good night's sleep before the speech

When You Speak

- Do not worry that the audience will readily pick up signs of nervousness. Most of the nervousness that you feel is not visible to the audience.

- Communicate in a conversational style. Try to use gestures and facial expressions that you regularly make use of in conversation.

- Slow your rate of delivery. When speakers become anxious, they often speak at a faster rate, resulting in increased nervousness.

- Concentrate on getting your message out. You do not need to perform; you need to communicate.

- Remember that the audience does not know what you plan to do during the speech. They will be slow to pick up on any mistake. Since they do not know exactly what you planned, it is easier to make adjustments during the speech without jeopardizing your objectives.

Regardless of which methods you choose to manage your nervousness, none are as effective as being well prepared. Preparation is the number one way to reduce speech anxiety, because the more time and effort you put into the speech the better you will feel about it. To further assist you in dealing with speech anxiety, visit the department website listed in your syllabus for additional speech anxiety resources.

Developing Confidence and Credibility

Your confidence and credibility as a speaker will have an impact on how successful you are in achieving your objectives. Overall, people are perceived as confident, credible sources when they are judged as competent and trustworthy. You can enhance both your confidence and credibility by doing the following:

- Be prepared to deliver your speeches on the assigned date

- Be on time for assigned speech dates

- Dress appropriately

- Check on the correct pronunciation of names and terms before the speech

- Anticipate the potential responses of the audience to your message

- Thoroughly research your topic; know the material!

- Report accurately on the topic being discussed

- Give proper credit to sources, and cite information correctly

- Effectively organize your speech

- Practice your speech thoroughly

Photo provided by John William Haas

Looking the Part

When you deliver a speech in this course, you are expected to dress appropriately. It will enhance your credibility and you will feel more confident as a speaker. This does not mean that you must wear formal business attire. However, it does mean that the following items are **unacceptable** to wear when delivering an **assigned, scheduled** speech:

- Shorts

- Jeans

- T-shirts

- Shirts with illustrations or writing

- Hats or bandanas

- Athletic apparel (jerseys, sweats, and so on)

- Torn or dirty clothing

- Sunglasses on your head or around your neck

- Revealing clothing

CHAPTER 4

You will be expected to wear business casual clothing when delivering an assigned speech. The only exception will be if you are using yourself as a visual aid and dressing the part of your speech. Research on this point is clear: if you do not look the part you will have less confidence in yourself as a speaker. In addition, you will be viewed as a less credible source if you do not look the part.

The School of Communication Studies maintains online resources that deal with speech anxiety. These resources can be accessed at *http://cmst.cci.utk.edu/content/speech-anxiety*.

Key Terms/Concepts to Know

Communication apprehension

Speech anxiety

Trait anxiety

State anxiety

Causes for speech anxiety

Problem thought patterns

Methods of managing speech anxiety

Self-perceptions

Competence

Physiology

Developing confidence and credibility

References

Bonner, S.F. (1977). *Education in ancient Rome: From the elder Cato to the younger Pliny*. New York: Routledge.

Millman, D. (2014). Peaceful heart, warrior spirit. Retrieved September 2, 2014 from *http://www.peacefulwarrior.com/*

CHAPTER 5

THE FIRST SPEECH

CHAPTER OBJECTIVES

This chapter is designed to help you understand:

- The public speaking process

- The basic components for preparing and delivering a speech

- Topic selection

- Speech objectives

- The basics of outlining

- The basics of speech delivery

Photo provided by John William Haas

A question that is frequently asked in a public speaking class involves how to plan for and deliver your first speech. You may be asking yourself, what am I supposed to do about (take your pick of topics) since that will not be covered until midway through the semester? For many, the concern is that there has not been enough content covered about how to prepare and deliver a speech in order to perform well and receive a good grade. Our goal with this chapter is to provide you with key information that will allow you to prepare and deliver your first speech. We will expand our discussion of each of the topics in the following chapters of the textbook.

CHAPTER 5

Selecting the Topic

Your first speech may require you to select a topic for the presentation. For many, this is the single most difficult part of preparing for a presentation. Speech teachers frequently hear comments such as, "I don't know what to talk about." Consider the following when selecting a topic:

- What do you know a good bit about?

- What do you feel strongly about?

- What are the topics of public conversation?

- What catches your imagination?

Simply put, select a topic that you know about, feel strongly about, or that captures your imagination. It will be more difficult to prepare and deliver a sound speech if you know little about the topic or if you have no interest in the topic.

Establishing Goals

Once you have selected a topic (or a topic is assigned), begin by identifying your goals. While broad goals may be rather easily identified (e.g., to persuade or to inform), it is important that you construct *specific* objectives. Specific objectives provide clear direction when preparing for the presentation and provide a better yardstick by which to measure the success of the presentation.

VAGUE	SPECIFIC
"I want people to learn more about me."	"I want to inform the audience of the three traits I possess that have shaped my life."

Developing a clear objective increases the probability that you will achieve your goal.

A final point on constructing objectives: make your goals realistic. The purpose statement should be attainable. Thus, depending on the setting (limited time, etc.), a realistic objective may be, "I want to inform the audience about the two traits that I possess that have shaped my life."

Gathering Information

After you have identified your goals, you need to begin gathering the information needed to attain the objectives. When selecting this information, you must consider your audience. Different audiences will require different kinds of information. Thus, you need to consider all of the following when gathering this information:

- Who will be in the audience?

- What is their level of knowledge concerning this topic?

- What, if any, attitudes do they hold toward this topic?

- What will the setting be like (the physical layout of the room, time of day, etc.)?

- How will audience members define this occasion?

- What are the possible objections audience members may have about my objectives, my treatment of the topic, etc.?

The information you gather should be driven by these concerns. By considering these issues, you will be able to adapt your message to the understandings, needs, and concerns of audience members.

Outlining the Information

There are several basic organizational patterns. The organizational pattern that you select for the speech should be driven by the goal of the presentation. The patterns that often lend themselves to informative presentations include topical and chronological. A topical organizational pattern works well when discussing separate topics that are held together by a central theme. For example, a topical pattern may be organized in the following way:

- Goal: To inform my audience of the three factors that lead to success in college

- Main Points:

  - Setting goals

  - Motivation

  - Obtaining internships

A second pattern often used to organize a speech involves a chronological pattern of organizing. When using this pattern the speaker organizes the content of the presentation according to time. This form is very useful when describing a process as you will likely wish to start with the beginning of the process and move forward in time to the completion of the process.

The patterns used most often in persuasive presentations include a cause–effect pattern and a problem–solution pattern. A cause–effect pattern shows that certain events have happened or will happen as a result of certain circumstances. Thus, the body of the presentation is organized around two major points: the cause(s) and the effect(s). The problem–solution pattern is usually used when the speaker is proposing some kind of change. When you use this pattern, describe the problem and reveal how your solution will solve the problem. In a situation where several solutions are possible but you advocate a particular one, make sure you indicate how the other solutions are not as adequate as the one you propose.

CHAPTER 5

When considering which of the major points to emphasize (for example, cause or effect), consider how the audience is likely to react. Focus more of the presentation on the point the audience is least likely to understand or agree with rather than on points of agreement. To achieve your objectives, you must overcome the misunderstandings and/or objections of audience members.

Introductions, Conclusions, and Transitions

INTRODUCTIONS

Introductions serve several functions: to capture the listeners' attention, to preview the body of the presentation, to set the proper tone for the topic and setting, and to give the audience a reason for listening. You may use several different types of openings. For example, you may begin by asking a question ("Would you continue to spend money on technology that can't meet our current needs, much less our future needs?"), providing a key piece of factual/statistical information (provided this information is significant to the audience, it will give them a reason for listening), or making a startling statement ("If current trends continue, TV commercials will replace physicians as the primary source of information about health-related technology.").

CONCLUSIONS

Conclusions serve several functions—summarize the presentation, point to the future, and emphasize what, if any, action needs to be taken.

TRANSITIONS

Transitions inform the audience we are changing topics or main points. Transitions between sections of the speech promote clarity by making explicit relationships between major points, keep listeners interested, and emphasize major ideas.

Constructing Visual Aids

Visual aids are particularly useful when making technical presentations. The following guidelines will help you to construct effective visual aids.

- Keep the visual aid as simple as possible

- Use contrasting colors (e.g., black and white, red and white, etc.)

- Balance the information in the visual (the right side of the visual should not contain significantly more information than the left side)

- Make sure the visual aid is large enough to be seen by all audience members

- Your visuals will communicate a great deal about you. If you wish to be taken as a professional, make sure your visual aids are prepared professionally.

Delivery

An extemporaneous form of delivery is the most effective. This form of delivery requires that the speaker *NOT* read from a manuscript or have memorized the speech. With an extemporaneous form of delivery, the speaker is sufficiently prepared and knowledgeable of the topic so that only limited assistance from notes is needed to make the presentation. Using this form of presentation allows the speaker to maintain eye contact with the audience in order to assess how the message is being received. Thus, the speaker is able to adapt to the audience during the presentation.

Effective delivery is characterized by naturalness and a conversational quality. Delivery which does not call attention to itself (unusual hand gestures, etc.) is natural. This allows the audience to focus on the message. Delivery that conveys a sense of interaction between the speaker and the audience may be described as having a conversational quality. Few people enjoy lectures. Most individuals prefer to be involved in a conversation. Thus, it is important to react to what the audience is telling you nonverbally.

Specific elements of effective delivery include:

- Direct eye contact

- Effective use of voice (volume, rate of speaking, pitch, articulation, and use of pauses)

- Good posture

- Effective hand gestures

- Effective facial expressions (i.e., consistent with the verbal message)

- Appropriate dress

Photo provided by John William Haas

Use of Visuals

- Visual aids should only be visible when in use.

- Do not talk to the visual aid; direct your attention toward the audience.

- If several visuals are used, number them by order of use.

- Become familiar with any equipment needed for the use of the visuals *prior* to the presentation.

- If using handouts:

    - Pass out the information at the end of the presentation if possible; and

    - If it is necessary to pass out the information during the presentation, allow audience members time to become familiar with it before proceeding.

- Prepare for the possibility that the visual aid can't be used (equipment failure, etc.).

CHAPTER 5

The ability to speak confidently and convincingly in public is increasingly tied to career development. Communication skills consistently rank among the top qualities that employers seek. Effective communication skills are linked to important individual outcomes such as upward mobility, positive performance evaluations, and job level. Moreover, few experiences will provide a person with a greater sense of empowerment than truly connecting with an audience. Unfortunately, for many people delivering a speech is as much fun as a trip to the dentist. Hopefully, the following tips may make this experience more pleasant:

TIP ONE

Identify your objective(s) for the presentation. It is surprising how often speakers have only a fuzzy idea of what they are seeking to accomplish. Construct clear, measurable objectives for the presentation so that you can assess the extent to which you succeeded.

TIP TWO

The single most important thing that you can do to deliver an effective presentation is to prepare. Nothing substitutes for preparation. Prepared speakers know their material, have anticipated how the audience might respond, and experience less nervousness.

TIP THREE

Make use of an extemporaneous style of delivery. This style of delivery requires that the speaker be prepared, make limited use of notes, and maintain eye contact with the audience. With an extemporaneous style of delivery the speaker prepares an outline that will serve to keep him or her on track and avoid the problems associated with memorizing or reading from a manuscript.

TIP FOUR

Adapt your message to the audience. People are persuaded or informed on the basis of what they value, believe, and understand—not on the basis of what the speaker values, believes, or understands. This does not mean that you change your goal for the presentation. Rather, adjust your message for each audience so that you are more likely to achieve your goal(s).

TIP FIVE

Limit your use of visual aids. Far too often visual aids are used as a substitute for the speaker. It is the speaker, not the visual aids, that determines whether the goals for the speech are achieved.

Key Terms/Concepts to Know

Selecting a topic	Patterns of organizing
Establishing goals	Topical
Transitions	Chronological
Visual aids	Cause–effect
Delivery	Problem–solution

UNIT 2

PUBLIC SPEAKING COMPONENTS

CHAPTER 6

SELECTING A TOPIC AND PURPOSE

CHAPTER OBJECTIVES

This chapter is designed to help you understand:

- How to select a topic for a speech

- How to create general and specific purpose statements

- How to develop central ideas

In the previous chapter we provided you with a capsulized version of how to select a topic and craft a purpose statement. In this chapter, we provide a more detailed view of how this process works.

As you begin the speech making process, you should begin by choosing a broad topic and continue this process by narrowing the topic until it is manageable within the setting for the speech (time limits, nature of the audience, etc.). Following topic selection, the next task is to write a specific purpose statement. As you continue through this section, use the following model to refer to the stages of this process. Notice that you will begin the process with a broad topic and develop a narrower approach to covering the topic in your speech.

Photo provided by John William Haas

CHAPTER 6

Topic: Ebola Virus

General purpose: To inform

Specific purpose: To inform my audience of the two primary ways people contract the Ebola virus.

Central idea: The two major ways of contracting the Ebola virus include physical contact with an infected person or contact with an infected surface or needle.

©Hayden-McNeil, LLC

Selecting a Topic

The first step in the speech making process is selecting the broad subject of the speech. Generally, this step is thought of as topic selection. There is no such thing as the "perfect topic." Thus, try not to dwell on this decision to the point that you are not using time wisely or that you become indecisive.

Your success with this step depends on how you approach the topic. Select a topic that you find interesting and/or feel strongly about. Avoid trivial topics. Instead, choose a topic that is worth hearing about and has value for both you and the audience. When your goal is to inform, choose a topic that is relevant to your audience. Think about what your audience needs to learn. When speaking to persuade, choose a topic that you feel strongly about that involves more than one viewpoint. When considering a speech topic, begin brainstorming for ideas using the following criteria.

FOCUS ON WHAT YOU KNOW

Draw upon your personal experiences when you begin the brainstorming process to select a topic. Whether you believe it or not, you know a lot. You have a wealth of experiences that others do not possess. Consider topics that will allow you to build on your current knowledge of the topic. Do not, however, choose a familiar topic because you think it will be less work. You will find that no matter how much knowledge you possess on a topic, it will require research since you must gather what will work for this audience—not for you. In fact, most students who select a topic about which they are knowledgeable are presented with an additional challenge. When you know a great deal about a subject, it is often difficult to relate to others with little or no knowledge of the topic. For example, an experienced photographer presenting an informative speech on how to photograph landscapes may struggle to relate to an audience with no photography experience. Speakers familiar with a topic tend to deliver speeches with too much technical information for the less experienced listener.

FOCUS ON WHAT CAPTURES YOUR IMAGINATION

You may want to consider choosing a topic that you are interested in and want to learn more about. Your interest in this type of topic may be sparked by a news report or by what you observe on a day-to-day basis. Use this opportunity to expand your knowledge.

FOCUS ON WHAT YOU CARE ABOUT

Each of us cares about issues, people, places, and ideas. Consider what you feel strongly enough about that warrants sharing with your classmates. This should be the case, especially in selecting a persuasive topic. If you do not care about what you are asking them to believe or do, it will make the process more tedious for you and make it obvious to your audience that the content is not very important to you.

FOCUS ON CURRENT ISSUES

Select a topic for either the informative or persuasive speech that involves a current event here on campus, in your town, state, and nation or around the world. Current affairs are very relevant for your classmates to know, especially if it will impact them, where they live, on a personal level. Busy college students may find it difficult to keep up-to-date with what is going on in the news.

You will probably find that many of the topics generated from this brainstorming activity will overlap. However, continue brainstorming until you have generated at least twelve separate topics (three for each category) without overlap. From this list of topics, consider which one you can most readily turn into an informative or persuasive speech.

General Purpose

The general purpose is the broad-based goal of a speech and is usually made clear to the speaker when he/she is invited or assigned to deliver a speech. The five general purposes of a speech are to inform, persuade, entertain, introduce, and inspire. The first two tend to involve scholarly speeches while the others are often most appropriate for special occasion speeches. Keep in mind that speakers are often confronted with situations in which they must pursue more than one general objective. For example, when delivering a persuasive speech to an audience with little or no knowledge of the topic, the speaker will find it necessary to inform the audience about the topic as well as persuade them to accept a particular viewpoint.

Specific Purpose

The specific purpose is a single, clear phrase that focuses on only one aspect of your topic. It should state precisely what you hope to accomplish in the speech. That is, the specific purpose should be stated in such a way that the goal is observable and measurable. For example, if your specific purpose is to persuade each audience member to donate $100 to the Red Cross, you have a clear way to observe or measure the extent to which you achieved your objective. Moreover, the specific purpose statement is useful because it forces you to zero in on one aspect of your broad topic. You will have time in a four-to-six or five-to-seven minute speech to talk about a limited

Got Purpose?

CHAPTER 6

number of main points. Thus, you will not be able to share everything you know about the topic. Narrowing the topic to a manageable size will allow you to better determine what needs to be discussed.

The purpose statement will drive how you prepare for the speech as well as how you will deliver the speech. Simply put, preparation and delivery must be focused on achieving the specific purpose. If the specific purpose is not clear, there is no guide for you to follow on how to research, organize, or prepare in general. Use the following example below of a specific purpose statement to write one of your own.

SPECIFIC PURPOSE STATEMENT

"To inform my audience about the five stages of relationship development"

- The sentence is crafted as a statement, not a question.

- The statement always begins with the general purpose: "To inform…." or "To persuade…."

- The topic should always be at the end of the statement (in this case, relationship development).

- The number of main points to be covered in the speech are identified (in this case five major points since there are five stages of relationships).

SPECIFIC PURPOSE GUIDELINES

After developing the specific purpose statement, follow the guidelines below:

- **It must be consistent with the general purpose.** The topic and specific purpose must meet the requirements of the assignment. That is, if the general purpose is to inform, avoid any content that involves persuasion. To avoid persuasive content, do not use words such as failing, benefits, advantages, dangers, and so on. These words, when used in the specific purpose, will direct the speech toward persuasion. In addition, some topics tend to be better suited to persuasive speeches than informative. For example, topics that involve some degree of controversy (you will find contradictory information when gathering information), such as global warming, seem better suited to persuasive presentations. After you have written your specific purpose, ask yourself the following question: Will I want to take the extra step to ask my audience to believe or do something? If the answer is yes, go back and make changes to keep the purpose informative.

- **It must be able to be accomplished in the time allotted.** Your purpose should be sufficiently narrowed so that it can be achieved in the time available for the informative speech as well as the persuasive speech assignment. Avoid the common mistake of

Speak with a clear purpose

developing specific purpose statements that require more than the allotted speech time to achieve. Far too often, students recognize late in the preparation process that they seek to accomplish more than can be accomplished in the time allotted.

- **It must be relevant to my audience.** You must consider your audience when choosing the topic to be addressed in the speech. Specifically, what do they need or want to learn about the topic based on their knowledge and interest level? You are not building a generic speech. Instead, you are tailoring it to the specific members of your audience. Seek to present information and/or arguments that are relevant to the values and experiences of this audience.

- **It must not be trivial.** Make sure that you do not choose a purpose that has little significance to your listeners. The audience will have little interest in a message that lacks relevance.

- **It must not be too technical.** Do not choose a purpose that is highly specialized unless the audience has expertise with the topic. In addition, consider the amount of time you have available to discuss a complex topic.

Central Idea

The central idea of a speech is a concise, one-sentence statement that makes clear what the speech is about. This concise statement is expected to include the main points of the presentation. The central idea is always based on the specific purpose and is shared with the audience at the end of the introduction. The goal of sharing this information with the audience is to preview the main points.

Photo provided by John William Haas

- **Central Idea:** The two major ways of contracting the Ebola virus include physical contact with an infected person or contact with an infected surface or needle.

Key Terms/Concepts to Know

Topic selection

General purpose

Specific purpose

Specific purpose guidelines

Central idea

CHAPTER 6

STUDENT NOTES

ANALYZING THE AUDIENCE

CHAPTER OBJECTIVES

This chapter is designed to help you understand:

- How to adapt your message to the audience

- Audience-centeredness

- Egocentrism

- How to determine audience interest and relevance

- The key factors involved in analyzing your audience

- How to gather audience information

- How to adapt to audience feedback

Photo provided by John William Haas

Adapting a message to its intended listener is something all of us do every day. For example, if you are informing your grandmother about the courses you are taking you would use different terminology from that which you would use with your friends. If you were persuading your parents to loan you money you would use different strategies between your mother and father. Separate arguments would be required to ask different instructors to raise your grade. In this course you will be expected to adapt your speech to a specific group of people (your classmates). Remember, you will not construct a generic speech. The practice of adapting your messages to the audience should continue after you complete this course. In fact, every speech you deliver should be adapted to the specific audience you plan to address.

When you analyze your audience, you will gather information about their attitudes, demographic characteristics, interest in the speech event, and knowledge of the speech topic. You will make use of this information to prepare for the speech as well as to adapt your message during the presentation.

Audience-Centeredness

One way to understand how speakers approach the public speaking process is in terms of egocentrism and audience-centeredness. **Egocentrism** suggests that the speaker simply expresses his or her views in terms of his or her own interests, values, beliefs, and experiences, regardless of the nature of the audience. Effective speakers recognize that this is not an effective way of approaching the audience. Receivers understand messages in terms of their own values, beliefs, and experiences. The self-centered speaker runs the risk of speaking about a topic in terms that receivers cannot relate to and runs the risk of losing their credibility. As discussed earlier, don't confuse egocentrism with ethnocentrism.

In addition, effective speakers understand that members of the audience are also egocentric. That is, members of the audience understand messages in terms of their own interests, values, beliefs, and experiences regardless of the nature of the speaker. They want to know what's in it for them and how the information is useful to their own lives. Since audience members think in their terms, effective speakers include the kind of information that receivers can relate to and understand.

In this course, you are expected to embrace an audience-centered view of public speaking. **Audience-centeredness** means that you adapt your message to the needs, interests, values, and beliefs of the receivers. This does not mean that your goals are determined exclusively by the audience. Rather, it means that you must develop messages that are designed to achieve your objectives in terms that are relevant to the interests, values, beliefs, and experiences of receivers. The reason it is so vital for a speaker to be audience-centered is because we are aware that audiences are indeed egocentric.

Audience Relevance and Interest

When preparing your speech, it is essential to understand how to make your information both relevant and interesting to your audience. **Interest** is simply holding the audience's attention. **Relevance** is the application of the information to the listeners. Audience members want to know how the information you are giving them is useful to their lives. Your information can be interesting but have no usefulness to your audience, or it can be something that the audience needs to know but is boring to listen to. You will need to find a way to be both relevant and interesting. The introduction of your speech will require a **relevance statement** that outwardly conveys why the audience should listen and why they need to know this information. This single sentence will inform the audience of how the topic/information is useful to them and how it can apply to their life. This single sentence should appear in the introduction of your speech.

Examining Your Audience

Learning about your audience is best accomplished by asking questions about them. Specifically, you should identify:

- Who will be in the audience?

- Why are they here?

- What is their knowledge level on the topic?

- What is their interest level on the topic?

- What attitude(s) do they hold toward the topic, the setting, and the speaker?

- How have they responded to speeches in the past about similar topics, in similar settings, and with similar speakers?

WHO WILL BE IN THE AUDIENCE?

Determining the audience composition will involve the use of demographic information. **Demographic variables** are characteristics of populations that can be used to segment or divide the population into groups. Demographic variables that speakers commonly seek information about include age, sex, race, ethnic background, socioeconomic status, religion, and group membership. The possible list of demographic factors is extensive, so it will be important for you to use sound judgment as to the list of factors you examine. For example, when preparing for a speech in your public speaking class, the kind of demographic variables that can be used to divide up the audience members would include major or class standing (freshman, and so on). However, this kind of demographic information will not be relevant for other audiences. It would not make sense to segment or divide a group of nursing home residents on the basis of the same demographic variables.

Effective speakers realize that all audience members do not respond the same way to a message. In part, different responses to a speech are the result of demographic factors. Gathering demographic information prior to the speech will assist you in two important ways. First, you will be able to gather the information necessary to achieve your speaking goals with this audience. The information you need to support your objectives when speaking to your classmates will be different from the information needed to support the same objectives in a speech to business associates. Second, you will be better able to anticipate the possible objections audience members may have to your goals. For example, a proposal to change admission standards to the College of Communication and Information may receive a different response from freshmen that have not been admitted to the College than seniors who have been admitted to a communication major.

When attempting to determine the demographic variables that are most or least important in navigating your speech content, you must look at what identifies the majority of the audience. For example, if your audience has a large age range or they are half men and half women, age or sex will not be important demographic factors to consider.

My speech was a complete success. The **audience** *was a failure.*

—Anonymous

WHY ARE THEY HERE?

People participate in public speaking situations for different reasons. The people in the audience may be attending the presentation because they have an interest in the topic, they may be required to attend, or they may receive some benefit from attending the speech. Answering the question of why people will attend the speech is necessary to prepare adequately. The information you need to support your objectives in a speech delivered to an audience of students required to attend class will be different from the information needed to support a speech with the same objective delivered to a church congregation.

WHAT IS THEIR KNOWLEDGE LEVEL ON THE TOPIC?

Audience members will have different levels of knowledge about your topic. Knowledgeable, well-informed audience members will require the speaker to make use of different kinds of information to achieve his/her objectives than less knowledgeable, less well-informed audiences. More often than not, speakers tend to overestimate what the audience knows and share information with the audience that is too technical because of the misjudgment. You cannot assume that the audience knows as much as you do either prior to or after your research. You have to find out how much each of them already knows so you have a better idea of what information to include and where to begin explaining.

WHAT IS THEIR INTEREST LEVEL ON THE TOPIC?

Similarly, the level of interest that audience members have in the topic should influence the kind of material that you include/exclude. Even though you have already narrowed your topic by writing a specific purpose, you need to discover what sub-topics/specific information your audience is most curious about learning. Again, you cannot assume that the audience will find the information as interesting as you find it.

WHAT ATTITUDES DO THEY HOLD TOWARD THE TOPIC?

An attitude may be thought of as a predisposition or evaluation toward someone or something. People's attitudes vary in intensity, and may range from a highly positive to a highly negative predisposition toward someone or something in their world. Moreover, the audience may be united or they may be divided in terms of the attitudes that they hold. It is commonly recognized that attitudes influence behavior. You can be certain that audience attitudes will play a central role in whether you achieve the speech objectives. The audience will hold attitudes about several different features of the speaking event. Audience members will hold attitudes toward the topic and purpose of the presentation. The audience will also hold attitudes toward the speaker, members of the audience, and the setting for the speech.

Answering the attitude question will provide you with direction for how to prepare the speech. If the audience holds a negative attitude toward you or your topic, what kind of information will you need to gather to achieve your objective(s)? The information you will need to gather to support your speaking objectives with an audience that holds

> *We can complain because rose bushes have thorns, or rejoice because thorn bushes have roses.*
>
> —Abraham Lincoln

a positive attitude toward the topic will be different from the kind of information necessary to achieve your objective with an audience that holds a negative attitude toward the topic. With the first group, you need to gather information designed to reinforce existing attitudes. With the second group, you need to gather information designed to bring about attitude change.

HOW HAVE THEY RESPONDED IN THE PAST?

In this course, you will have the opportunity to observe how audience members respond to speakers. What were speakers saying or doing to evoke a strong reaction (positive or negative) from the audience? What were speakers saying or doing when they generated little, if any, response from the audience? You will not always have the opportunity to view how your audience reacts outside of class to other speakers, but make use of this information when it is available.

Gathering Audience Information

You can gather information about your audience from a variety of sources. While a more detailed discussion of gathering supporting materials for your speech appears later in your textbook, it is useful to note here the methods of gathering audience-related information:

- Conducting library research to determine how groups similar to this audience (based on demographic characteristics) view your topic.

- Interviewing the individuals or groups responsible for arranging the public speaking event. To whom are they promoting the event? Who received invitations? Who do they expect to attend?

- **Administering a survey-questionnaire to audience members**. This method of gathering information may not always be possible for speeches delivered outside of class. However, when the opportunity exists, you should make use of this opportunity to gather information from the audience. For your informative and persuasive speech, seek to gather as much information about your audience as possible including demographic information, knowledge and interest level, and attitudes toward your topic. When developing a survey-questionnaire, ask only the questions needed to gather relevant information. Since this is the method you will use to learn about your audience, the following types of questions may be helpful to create your own survey-questionnaire for class. Each of the following types of questions are used to gather different types of information about audience members.

  - **Forced choice questions**. These questions are straightforward with opposing answers. These questions gather general information rather than specific information that may be necessary for the development of your speech. Make sure that you include a third response such as "do not know," "not sure," or "no opinion."

- Have you ever driven a car under the influence of alcohol?

Yes ___ No ___ Not sure ____

Fixed questions are not effective for finding the level of knowledge the audience member has about the topic since, even though the respondent's name is not included, many do not want to admit that they do not know something. Fixed questions are more effective for persuasive speeches that attempt to discover whether the listeners already believe or do what you are asking of them.

- **Likert Scale items or questions**. These items (statements) or questions are useful for determining attitudes the audience has toward a topic. Named after the person who developed this type of scale (psychologist Rensis Likert), this way of measuring people's attitudes and perceptions is widely used. In fact, this is the type of scale that students use in completing evaluations of their teachers.

  - I always come prepared for class.

Never	**Seldom**	**Sometimes**	**Often**	**Always**
1	2	3	4	5

Like the example above, all scale questions should have an odd number of responses, giving respondents a middle choice that indicates neither agreement nor disagreement.

- **Open-ended questions**. The answers to these questions usually provide the best indicator of how much your audience knows (knowledge level) about the topic. Open-ended questions are also an effective method for gathering information from the respondent that you may not have considered. However, this information is the most time-consuming to gather. Examples of open-ended questions appear below:

  - Describe what you experience when delivering a speech.

  - Describe your views on global warming.

Beginning an open-ended question with the word "describe" is among the most effective ways of getting the respondent to provide you with detailed answers.

- **Demographic questions**. As discussed, demographic variables are important factors to consider when delivering a speech. For a few demographic variables such as age, you may not need to gather information since the members of the audience tend to be the same age range. However, depending on your topic, you may need to determine demographic factors such as group membership or socioeconomic status. This will help you determine their interests, knowledge level, or attitudes. These questions are best administered at the end of your survey.

Preparing for the Setting

Because the setting impacts the speech, consider how you can adapt the speech so as to achieve your speaking objectives. When preparing your speech, consider the following about the setting:

- **The speech location.** Speaking opportunities and challenges vary considerably based on the location of the speech. For example, an outdoor location presents a speaker with a different set of opportunities and challenges than an indoor location. Consider what it took the audience to make it to the location and what you will have to do to adapt to this site yourself.

- **The physical layout of the room.** The room layout will influence how the speaker establishes the kind of relationship he/she is seeking with the audience. If there is a lectern (podium), you will need to determine whether using it is necessary or advantageous. If the space permits, you will want to stand in the front and center of the room. This is so you are the focus and everyone in the audience can see you. In addition, the layout influences the kinds of visual aids a speaker selects for the speech, since visual aids must be visible to all audience members.

- **Physical interference in or around the room**. Possible interference, such as room temperature or people talking in surrounding rooms, needs to be considered when preparing for a speech. Extremes in temperature will impact negatively on your speech. Prior to the speech, you would want to check to see if the room temperature can be adjusted. If not, be prepared to adjust your speech based on the impact of room temperature or noise.

- **The time of day for the speech.** If you have taken an 8:00 a.m. class, you realize that audience members are not always motivated to listen to the speaker, because of the time of day. If possible, select the time for the speech that you feel audience members will be most receptive to the speech. If that is not possible, consider how the time of day will impact on the willingness of audience members to attend to your speech. For example, speaking right before lunch may make for some hungry, distracted listeners.

- **The audio-visual equipment**. A problem that is increasingly encountered by speakers concerns audio-visual equipment. Too often speakers using presentation software such as PowerPoint® find that their equipment, disks, or cables are not compatible with the technology available at the location for the speech. Whenever possible, conduct a test run on the equipment at the facility where the speech will be delivered to determine system compatibility. DO NOT assume that your computer, disks, or cables are compatible with the technology available at the location for the speech or that someone will have it ready for you. In class, bring your presentation at least one class time prior to your speech day so you can make sure it works properly. A second strategy to avoid audio-visual problems is to bring your own equipment. For example, extension agents for the University of Tennessee bring

Photo provided by John William Haas

Photo provided by John William Haas

to the location of the speech all of the equipment needed for a PowerPoint® presentation, including laptop computers, projectors, extension cords, power strips, and adapters for two-prong wall outlets. If your success hinges on audio-visual equipment that works, learn what the setting has available for speakers.

Adapting to Audience Feedback

As previously discussed, regardless of the time and effort devoted to audience analysis in preparation for the speech, it is essential to continue the analysis process during the speech. Even well-prepared speakers can be surprised by a range of factors from unexpected guests in the audience to breaking news stories about your topic, to unexpected or disinterested responses on the part of the audience. One example of adapting to audience feedback would come during your speech if you see confused or inquisitive looks on the face of your listeners. You would want to stop where you are in your speech, go back and clarify your last point instead of ignoring the nonverbal feedback you are receiving and continuing.

The confidence to make changes in mid-speech will be strongly influenced by your level of preparation. Knowing the material gives you the confidence to be flexible with the speech outline, to omit or add information, to rearrange the order of information, or make unexpected use of stories and anecdotes. By presenting a speech extemporaneously, as mentioned earlier in your text, you will be able to do this effectively. Adapting to feedback takes practice, though. The more you speak in public the more comfortable you will be in veering off from what was previously planned when necessary, and thinking more quickly on your feet.

Photo provided by John William Haas

Adapting during the speech requires that you accurately diagnose the feedback provided by the audience. In many cases the need to adapt will be clear, based on the nonverbal behaviors of audience members. However, speakers are often unsure of what the audience is communicating. For example, it may not be clear to the speaker based on nonverbal cues whether the audience could not hear what was said or if they disagreed with the message. If you are in doubt, ask **comprehension questions**. This is a special kind of question that seeks feedback from the audience. For example, questions posed in conversational style by the speaker such as, "Does this make sense?" or "Would you like more information before we go on to the next topic?" following the description of a complex issue will help the speaker connect with the audience. If the audience members respond positively, the speaker continues with the presentation. If there does not appear to be an affirmative response to the question, the speaker needs to make a mid-course change, and restate and clarify the information for the audience. Asking questions is a very useful method of gathering feedback. Be cautious when asking questions, however, since a lengthy audience response may result in a much longer speech than assigned.

Effective speakers know that they must respond to what the audience is communicating whether the message is agreement or disagreement or disinterest. Consider the following question. How do you respond to people who ignore your messages? Probably not well. Few people respond positively to being ignored. By responding and adapting your message during the presentation, you communicate to the audience that you are aware of them and acknowledge their views.

Key Terms/Concepts to Know

Audience-centeredness

Egocentrism

Relevance statement

Examining your audience

Gathering audience information

Speech setting

Adapting to audience feedback

Comprehension questions

STUDENT NOTES

CHAPTER 8

GATHERING SUPPORT FOR THE SPEECH

CHAPTER OBJECTIVES

This chapter is designed to help you understand:

- The different types of information sources

- How to evaluate sources of information

- How to cite sources appropriately

- How to choose appropriate supporting information

- APA format

Photo provided by John William Haas

After you have selected the topic, established the purpose, and analyzed the audience, it is time to gather the information necessary to support your speech. Advances in information technology make it possible to easily access and explore an enormous body of literature on most any topic. In fact, there is often too much information available! In this chapter we seek to sort out how you can efficiently gather the information needed to support your speech objectives.

Regardless of the amount of knowledge you have on the topic, you must support all information in your speech with credible sources. As the speaker, you are a single source. You must locate other sources who provide support for your message. While you may use your own experiences and knowledge as examples to personalize your speech, your strongest support will come from other sources.

You will make use of several different kinds of sources in support of your presentation goals. Speakers often believe that sources are not necessary if they are knowledgeable of the subject. While it is expected that you be knowledgeable of the topic, a question that you should consider is whether other credible sources share your opinions. The audience will have much more confidence in a speaker if that speaker cites many credible sources on the topic.

In order to be successful in this course, it will be necessary to gather supporting material from the UT Libraries. The UT Libraries have developed a number of resources specifically for public speaking students that are designed to help you to gather information from appropriate sources. Specifically, these resources include tutorials, subject and course guides, and databases/indexes. The information that follows will help you better understand how to support your speech.

Source Criteria

Conducting an effective search will require that you make use of a variety of methods to gather information in support of your speech. Regrettably, many speakers rely too heavily on Web-based sources of information to support their speech objectives. As you will see, this is not a sound practice and may lead a speaker to perform poorly. Simply put, the audience will place more confidence in information gathered from multiple sources. Your speeches will require a variety of sources that are considered both **credible** and **current**. Review the course syllabus for specific criteria regarding the number and type of sources required for the informative and persuasive speeches.

CREDIBLE SOURCES

For the purposes of this course, the most credible source is a scholarly source. You are required to use scholarly sources for your speech assignments. A scholarly source is peer-reviewed. That is, the information in the article has undergone a blind review by more than one expert in that topic area in order to insure that the information in the article is credible.

In addition to scholarly or peer-reviewed articles, it is often appropriate to use credible sources of information that are not peer-reviewed. However, this information needs to be used more cautiously. Receivers often judge (correctly) that publications that do not pass through a review process are biased, not as credible, or not as likely to be accurate. If your topic is not scholarly, that is, it is a topic that has not been systematically studied (and there are very few such topics!), you should rely on other credible sources such as expert opinion in a related subject or others who have had previous experience with the topic. For example, if your informative speech involves an event such as a game day experience at a home football game, a journal article will most likely not be appropriate. Rather, you should interview experts such as the band director, sports broadcasters, and university administrators in charge of athletics in order to gather credible information. If your speech involves a concept, such as exercise, begin by finding studies (journal articles) conducted on the topic and follow up by interviewing trainers or other professionals. Other potential sources, such as a website, interview, or company brochures, are not considered scholarly but could be credible enough to use as a source if you follow the evaluation process discussed later in the chapter.

HOW DO I RECOGNIZE A PEER-REVIEWED JOURNAL?

- Visibly different from other publications

- Little or no advertising

- Little or no use of color

- Considerable use of footnotes

- Editorial board and editorial policies stated at the beginning of the journal

CURRENT SOURCES

The topic of your speech will dictate what a current, credible source will be for you. For example, a speech about World War II would possibly include sources prior to the war, during the war, and following the war. However, a topic such as nutrition and exercise will require current sources that report the most up-to-date information available. As you consider the worth of any source, be aware that certain types of sources are more current than others. That is, the information has been published or broadcast recently rather than a more distant point in time. Television, radio broadcasts, and Web-based news sources (if updated daily) are the most current sources of information. Published periodicals such as magazines are somewhat current in that they may be updated once a week or once a month. Journal articles are less current (these are typically published quarterly), but more current than books or reference sources such as encyclopedias.

Types of Sources

Different types of sources produce different kinds of information. You will need to utilize a variety of sources in order to gather a variety of materials. The more extensive your sources, the more credible your information. As mentioned previously, you should refer to your syllabus for the number and kind of sources required for your informative and persuasive speeches. Since the informative and persuasive speech assignments are scholarly in nature, an appropriate number of peer-reviewed sources are required for these speeches.

SCHOLARLY SOURCES

Scholarly sources of information generally include **peer-reviewed** publications such as **journal articles** you will find on the library databases. In general, a journal article reports the results of a study that has been conducted by researchers in the field to either answer a research question or to attempt to confirm a hypothesis. A peer-reviewed source has been subject to a "blind" review by other experts in the field to determine if the manuscript is worthy of publication. Since the material is anonymously reviewed prior to acceptance for publication, peer-reviewed publications are believed to be the most reliable sources of information. Examples of peer-reviewed journals include *The New England Journal of Medicine*, *Human Communication Research*, *The Academy of Management Review*, and *The Journal of Personality and Social Psychology*. Some of the **books** you will find in the UT Libraries, such as the *Communication Yearbook* series, are also peer-reviewed. Many books, however, are not peer-reviewed. The credentials of the author will help you determine how credible the source is. Books can be found by searching UT Libraries database.

In fact, most publications are not peer-reviewed. **Periodicals** that you may read regularly such as *Time*, *U.S. News and World Report*, *Psychology Today*, *The Knoxville News Sentinel* or other newspapers/ magazines are not peer-reviewed. Many newspaper and magazine articles are written by journalists or columnists who do not cite their sources. This does not mean that the information presented in these publications is necessarily inaccurate or that they are not credible.

Rather, you need to evaluate materials in terms of the level of confidence we assign to the publication. The more rigorous the review process prior to publication, the more confidence we have in the accuracy of the claims made by the author(s). It follows that receivers will have more confidence in the claims made by a speaker when the supporting material comes from peer-reviewed publications, which is the most credible source.

WEB-BASED SOURCES

An exclusive reliance on Web-based sources is not a sound practice. Web-based search engines such as Google or Yahoo will generate a vast number of websites associated with most any topic. However, the majority of these websites are of little or no value to a speaker in search of credible sources. In contrast to the use of a search engine, speakers often locate credible sources through the use of electronic databases maintained by the library.

A Web-based search engine or website operates in a very different way from a library database. A **citation database** (e.g., Social Sciences Citation Index) indexes or catalogues hundreds or thousands of journals that allows for virtually instant searching of topics or authors. Thus, databases act as reservoirs for a large number of articles that deal with a broad topic (e.g., communication or psychology or business) and are designed to simplify the search process. These types of citation databases are licensed to the library (for a substantial fee!) and are available for use by students and faculty with their Net ID and password.

While most websites are not considered scholarly sources, they can be considered credible if they make clear how their information was obtained. When using the Web, the domain of .gov, .org, or .edu is more credible than .com since a .com is easy to obtain by anyone.

While most websites are not considered scholarly sources, they can be considered credible if they report how their information was obtained. When using the Web, non-scholarly sources that offer a high degree of credibility include government websites (normally associated with the domain of .gov) or educational institutions (normally associated with the domain of .edu).

While Web-based information resources are available through the UT Libraries, it is certainly possible for you to conduct your own Web-based research. The Web is a marvelous tool that can be used to explore most any topic. We can safely say that the introduction of the Web in this information age has had a profound impact on how speakers research their topics. When finding websites, you may only use the site as a source if the following information is available:

- The author's name and credentials/expertise (researcher, physician, college professor, and so on) or the **sponsoring organization** that manages the website (Mayo Clinic, The Centers for Disease Control and Prevention, and so on) and

- The date the information was placed on the Web.

WHAT ARE WIDELY USED CITATION DATABASES?

- Web of Science

- Scopus

- Google Scholar

If the author's name, credentials, sponsoring organization, and date that the information was posted are not available, do not use the information. This is a "red flag" that the information may not be credible and/or current, or could be biased.

Conducting research on the Web for your speeches presents a number of potential problems. These potential problems include:

- **An overwhelming volume of information**. A popular search engine was used to explore three terms. First, we searched for sites that involve public speaking. The search engine returned a total of approximately 270,000,000 Web pages that referenced public speaking. A search for global warming turned up close to 206,000,000 Web pages. Finally, we asked the search engine to locate pages for the University of Tennessee. For this search, around 105,000,000 Web pages were identified. It is not practical (or even possible) to review all of these Web pages. Given the volume of Web pages on most topics, how do you locate the appropriate sites?

- **Problematic search strategies**. Let's begin with what not to do. Far too many people rely on the "first listed, first used" search strategy for Web research. That is, many people will make use of the first twenty to thirty listings regardless of their actual value as sources of information. A search strategy that involves using the first few listings for the search term will likely result in wildly inaccurate information that is not relevant to the purpose of the presentation, but happens to have something to do with global warming.

  When using the Web for research, your search strategy should include the advanced search options that more precisely target your search. Advanced search options are available on most search engines. These options will allow you to restrict the search to exact phrases, specific time frames, specific domains (highly important strategy on the Web), specific publications, or specific countries of origin. For example, a Google search for global warming turned up over 14 million Web pages. When using Google Advanced Search and restricting the search to only the domain ".gov," the search engine will limit the Web pages listed to those created by the U.S. government. When using the Web for research, your search strategy should include the advanced search options that more precisely target your search.

Photo provided by John William Haas

REFERENCE SOURCES

Reference sources include publications such as encyclopedias and dictionaries. In general, reference sources offer summarized information about a range of topics. While you may be familiar with popular brands of encyclopedias that cover a vast range of topics, many reference sources/encyclopedias exist that cover a narrower range of issues, such as the medical focus found in the *Johns Hopkins Medical Desk Reference*. This summarized information provides a good "jumping off" point for further inquiry. Thus, reference sources should not be both the beginning and the end point for your research.

Many people make use of Wikipedia as a source of information when looking to define terms. Simply put, this is not a good idea. **For the purposes of this course, Wikipedia is not an appropriate source of information.** As stated on the Wikipedia main page available at *http://en.wikipedia.org/wiki/Main_Page*, it is a "free encyclopedia that anyone can edit." Since the knowledge or expertise of the "editor" is unclear, Wikipedia is a less reliable source of information than refereed journals or other academic sources. If you are not sure what we mean by this, consider the following: How comfortable would you be if your physician consulted Wikipedia prior to prescribing a treatment for you? Would it be OK if your physician relied on the quality of the information about treatments for you that anyone can edit? Or, would you prefer that well-trained physicians review information before it is published?

INTERVIEWS/SURVEYS

Interviews and/or surveys are often used as a source to gather supporting materials for a speech. You may choose an expert in the field who researches the topic or someone who has had experience doing something discussed in your speech firsthand. Or, you may want to survey a group of people to gather more information. One advantage of using this method is that the information gathered from survey/interview respondents tends not to be available from any other source. However, a limitation of this method of gathering supporting material is that it can be a time-consuming, labor-intensive activity.

When preparing an **interview** with someone, the following tips should help:

- Find someone who is an expert in the field or has experience in your topic.

- Make an appointment with this person to interview him/her. A face-to-face interaction is always more effective than a phone or online interview, but either will be considered an interview.

- Find the "gaps" in your research where you may be missing support for ideas you want to share. This is a great way to begin constructing questions to ask this individual.

- Be on time for the meeting and only ask questions that will give you the information and support you will need for your speech.

- Always give the interviewee a chance to add any comments that were not discussed in the question/answer time. This may give you greater insight that you had not previously considered.

When developing a **survey** outside of class, use these following guidelines:

- Make sure that the information you gather cannot be obtained from other sources.

- A survey must include a cover page that explains the purpose of the project and what will happen with the data that is collected.

- The student conducting the survey for this course must follow the Human Subjects policies at the University of Tennessee.

- Make sure that the survey has a professional appearance.

- Recognize that response rates decline as survey length is increased, so keep it as brief as possible.

- Make sure that you safeguard the data collected and that individuals are not identified in the way you report the information. The name of a respondent should not be solicited nor reported.

BROCHURES/PAMPHLETS

Depending on your speech topic, there may be instances when you find it appropriate to use brochures or pamphlets as a source. These are usually printed by an organization and include information about some aspect of that organization. For example, if your speech is to persuade your audience to study abroad, you would want to gather pamphlets from the Programs Abroad Office here at UT for more information. In order to use a brochure or pamphlet as a source you must know the sponsoring organization that printed it and the date it was created/revised.

MOTION PICTURE/TELEVISION BROADCAST

Depending on your topic and purpose, there may be instances in which it will be useful to cite movies or television programs. For example, the documentary produced by Kenneth Burns entitled *The Civil War* may provide useful information taken from the interviews that are included in the film. News broadcasts can also be useful in supporting claims made in a speech. In addition, the content of movies and television shows is often useful to demonstrate that an issue is widely and commonly discussed.

Evaluating Sources

Not all sources are equally sound. In fact, many sources found on the Web or in a library may be biased or inaccurate. When weighing the value of an information source, consider the following criteria:

- **Primary vs. secondary sources**. One way to assess the value of information is to determine whether it is derived from a primary or secondary source. Simply put, a primary source involves the original words or work of the author(s). Primary sources are records of events as they are first described, without any interpretation or commentary. A primary source may also include sets of data, such as census statistics, that have been summarized, but not interpreted. Secondary sources, on the other hand, offer an analysis or a restatement of primary sources. They often attempt to describe or explain primary sources. Some secondary sources not only analyze primary sources, but use them to advance a particular opinion. For example, a primary source would include a transcript of a presidential speech that is available on the White House website. An editorial on that speech that appears in a local newspaper would be considered a secondary source.

Photo provided by John William Haas

- **Scholarly publications vs. popular press publications**. A second way to assess the value of information is to determine whether it is derived from a scholarly publication or a popular press publication. As discussed, a scholarly publication must pass through a review process to determine its worth for publication. Authors are expected to offer substantial support for the claims that are made in the article. Articles that appear in popular press publications do not pass through this type of review process. Thus, you should be less confident in the soundness of the information contained in articles that appear in the popular press. The following highlights differences between scholarly/peer-reviewed publications and popular press publications:

SCHOLARLY/ PEER-REVIEWED	POPULAR
Precise, specific information on a topic	More general information on a topic
Somewhat less current and timely	Somewhat more current and timely
Confidence in accuracy: High	Confidence in accuracy: Moderate to low
Sources cited	Generally lacks cited sources
Bias level: Low	Bias level: Potentially low to high
Target audience: Scholars in the field	Target audience: General public

- **Library databases vs. Web sources**. A third way to assess the value of information is to determine whether it is derived from a library database or from a Web-based search engine. Library databases offer systematic, reliable methods of identifying information as well as methods for determining the worth of the information. Web-based search engines offer no systematic, reliable methods of screening sources as to the quality of the information. In fact, if you created a website about public speaking today, it is possible that students at other schools across the globe would use your page as a source of information! Keep in mind that any person or group can develop a website on most any topic and electronically publish biased, distorted, or completely inaccurate information.

Choosing Supporting Material

Supporting material is just that—material that supports the purpose of your speech. Your goal in gathering supporting material is to find information that provides backing for the speech objectives. There are a variety of types of supporting material used by speakers to advance their objectives. The starting point in this process involves your specific purpose. All the material included in your speech should be directly related to the purpose. Information should be used only when it helps you achieve your objective. Effective speakers tend not to rely on a single type of supporting material, knowing that no one type of support will have the desired impact on all audience members. When gathering and selecting information to use in the speech, consider what kind of impact you need to achieve with this information. Also, realize that different pieces of information come from different types of sources. If you can recognize the type of source that is found, you will better understand the credibility and currency of the information. You will also know where to look for the supporting material you need. For example, if you need statistics to quantify an idea, you will learn that you can find them in journal articles but not in most books. The types of supporting material you will make use of in this course include facts, statistics, expert testimony, peer testimony, examples, stories, and personal experience.

FACTS

Facts involve information that can be demonstrated to be true and are regarded as beyond dispute. For example, we know now that the earth is round and that the earth revolves around the sun. Moreover, the source of the information for that fact can be examined. For example, it is a fact that the average high temperature in Knoxville during the month of August is 87°, according to the National Weather Service. This is a factual statement because it can be demonstrated to be true through examination of the source information. Facts can be found across many different types of sources. Because facts are not in dispute, they provide powerful support for a speaker. However, it is essential that the speaker avoid labeling nonfactual information as fact. Playing fast and loose with the facts will destroy your credibility as a speaker.

Most facts will not be found in journal articles, since each involves a single study conducted in one moment of time with one group of participants. Moreover, when reporting factual information, be cautious about making claims. If you report that something is "proven" then you are stating that this fact is true for all time. Few facts reach that level of certainty. It is best when reporting information to note that research suggests or that we have a great deal of confidence in a study result. Simply put, avoid the word "prove" because that may generate controversy among the audience members.

DID YOU KNOW...?

There are many fact-checker sites on the Web including:

- FactCheck.org
- PolitiFact.com
- The Fact Checker
- OpenSecrets.org
- Snopes.com
- TruthOrFiction.com

Table 8.1 *Paired Samples Statistics*[a]

		MEAN	N	STD. DEVIATION	STD. ERROR MEAN
Pair 1	pregroup	15.4223	779	5.23313	.18750
	postgroup	14.7997	779	4.92107	.17632
Pair 2	premeeting	16.2401	779	4.92960	.17662
	postmeeting	15.1592	779	4.77384	.17104
Pair 3	predyadic	14.3081	779	4.30968	.15441
	postdyadic	13.9332	779	4.11789	.14754
Pair 4	prepublic	20.7356	779	5.13012	.18381
	postpublic	18.4044	779	4.95735	.17762
Pair 5	preoverallCA	66.7060	779	16.24181	.58192
	postoverallcomapp	62.2965	779	15.60504	.55911

a. Are you male or female? = Female

STATISTICS

Statistics also have the potential to provide powerful support for a speaker. Statistics are usually generated through individual studies conducted to gather data on a certain subject. Therefore, they can be found in journal articles and in databases provided by the UT Libraries. Statistics are needed in your speech anytime it is necessary to quantify your ideas. For example, you would not want to state that something occurs "often" or that "many" people do something. That kind of statement is too vague and does not clarify the information for your audience. Instead, you should find statistical information that would assign a number to the frequency of the event so that it becomes real and tangible to the audience. Statistical information can be manipulated, however. In order to build speaker credibility, you must use statistics accurately and ethically. When used appropriately and skillfully, statistical information constitutes one of the most effective types of support for a speaker.

Statistical information can take one of two forms: Descriptive statistics or inferential statistics. **Descriptive statistics** describe some feature(s) of the participants involved in a study. For example, the statistical information generated from student evaluations of instruction available online are presented as descriptive statistics. This kind of statistical information generally takes the form of means (averages), percentages, or frequencies. Simply put, descriptive statistics describe a population (in this case, the students enrolled in a particular course) but do not claim to represent the views of the entire population (all students enrolled at the University of Tennessee).

Inferential statistics differ from descriptive statistics in one very important aspect. When using this kind of statistic, we seek to take information from a sample (2,000 registered voters) of a population (125,000,000 registered voters) and make inferences or claims about those same features in the entire population. As we discussed about the information derived from descriptive statistics, it is essential that you make appropriate and ethical use of information derived from inferential statistics. In particular, use caution about making claims that are based on the results of studies that make use of inferential statistics. Avoid the use of words such as "prove" when using statistics. Rather, make use of words such as the study "suggests" or "offers evidence" to support a specific point. Statistics must represent what they claim to measure and they must be gathered from reliable sources.

It is beyond the scope of this course to provide detailed instruction in statistics. However, if you need assistance with the proper use or interpretation of statistical information, the UT Statistical Consulting Center offers free consulting services to students. In addition, your library will provide you with assistance in locating statistical information for your speech.

EXPERT TESTIMONY

Effective supporting material may be gathered from the opinions of those recognized as experts on a topic. Experts are believed to possess a great deal of credibility by receivers because of some combination of experience, training, and education regarding the topic of interest. Two factors are important when making use of expert opinion. First, the people cited must be perceived as an expert by others who are judged to possess similar expertise. The author of a self-help book on nutrition that is universally rejected by professional nutritionists should not be cited as an expert in nutrition. Second, make sure that the expert is dealing with the topic with which he/she has expertise. A nutrition professional is not necessarily an expert on the issues surrounding global warming. Inappropriate or unethical use of expert opinion will diminish your credibility as a speaker. You must also make sure that you use testimony from unbiased sources. For example, you would not want to make a claim that one product is better than another by using the maker of the product as a source because it would not bring credibility to your claim. Instead, seek out an unbiased third-party to support your claim.

Expert testimony can be found in a secondary source, such as a periodical, that reported information from the original source's interview. You can also obtain expert testimony by conducting an interview with someone who researches or studies the topic. This testimony does not have to be quoted word-for-word, but may be paraphrased as long as the original idea is intact.

PEER TESTIMONY

Depending on your speech topic, you may need to find someone who has firsthand experience doing what it is you are talking about. For example, if your purpose is to inform your audience how to saddle a horse, then you would want to interview someone you know who has done it before. While expert testimony comes from someone who has been trained and has researched the topic, peer testimony comes from an individual who has firsthand experience seeing or doing it. Like expert testimony, this can be found in periodicals, websites, or an interview that you conduct with someone. If you have experience doing something you may include it as an example but find others who have similar experiences to use as sources and supporting material.

Photo provided by John William Haas

EXAMPLES

Examples can help a speaker clarify complex concepts. Examples as supporting material offer the advantage of helping receivers "visualize" the meaning of the message. They are used to clarify, reinforce, and condense your ideas. You may find examples in your sources or create your own. You may want to use brief examples from sources, in passing, to help you better illustrate main points for the audience. Sometimes, however, you will need to make use of **hypothetical examples**, which create an imaginary or fictitious situation by relating the scene or event directly to the audience. This type of example is best used when you are discussing an instance that may be difficult for your audience to grasp. Examples must be adapted to the audience, easily understood, vivid, and memorable.

STORIES

Stories are useful as supporting material to make a point and are, in essence, extended examples. Moreover, stories offer a memorable, entertaining method of conveying information. Dr. Andy Holt, former president of the University of Tennessee, was well known for his use of stories about economically distressed students in speeches seeking financial support for the University. When making use of stories as supporting material be certain that the audience will draw the "correct" lesson from the story. It would not have served Dr. Holt's purpose if receivers interpreted the story to mean that we admit too many financially distressed students to the University rather than the point that we need to strengthen our financial support for worthy, academically sound students. Make sure that when you tell a story in your speech, you keep it brief and practice how you will tell it since you do not have much time for these.

PERSONAL EXPERIENCE

Your personal experiences, if used appropriately, can provide compelling support for your objectives. Describing your experiences with the topic lends a real-life perspective to an issue that cannot be achieved through the use of facts or statistical information. In fact, speakers who do not include personal experience often create distrust within the audience and show a lack of credibility with their subject matter. When considering whether to include personal experiences in your speech, consider the following:

- Will your use of personal experience have the desired impact on the audience?

- How relevant are your personal experiences to this audience?

- How consistent are your personal experiences with other forms of supporting material?

- What are the potential consequences of revealing this information to this audience?

Citing Information

You are required to verbally document (cite) your sources of information in speeches. Simply put, you must give people credit for their ideas. Appropriate documentation enhances the credibility of the speaker. When you provide listeners with information about how you came by your facts, statistics, or testimony, they will have more confidence in the soundness of your ideas. When citing sources during your speech, provide enough information about the source so that listeners are clear on where you obtained the information. Since your sources must be credible and current, a citation must convince the audience that the source is credible and current.

You should think about this process as citing information (supporting material) rather than citing sources. Thinking only about citing sources will tempt you to seek the minimum number of required sources for the assignment. This will not serve you well in class or following your undergraduate experience. Most speeches call for multiple sources, and their use will strengthen the audience belief that the speaker is credible and competent. Make use of the following information when citing sources in your speech:

CITING INFORMATION

You **must** cite the information when:

- Directly quoting from a source verbatim (word-for-word)

- **Paraphrasing** (restating or summarizing a source's ideas in your own words)

- Borrowing from others' ideas on how to structure (or organize) the content of your speech

- Using the illustrations, diagrams, or graphs of others

You **do not** need to cite information in the following circumstances:

- Reporting your own original ideas

- Discussing ideas that are commonly held. **Common knowledge** is considered information that cannot be disputed, like facts. For example, people do not cite Copernicus as the source of information for statements suggesting that the Earth revolves around the sun. Moreover, it is commonly understood that World War II ended in 1945; no source citation is necessary to support that claim. One rule of thumb to follow is whether you "looked up" the information. If you were uncertain or unaware of the information before your trip to the library or the World Wide Web, make sure to cite the sources that you used. In addition, if you have heard the information from somewhere before or cannot explain how you know it, and it is not considered common knowledge, go find a source that does say it. When in doubt whether the information you have found is common knowledge—cite it.

HOW TO CITE INFORMATION

All citations

No matter what type of supporting material you take from the sources, all of the citations you create from them should include two items. Speech citations must first include the **date** of the source in order to let the audience know that the source is current. This will be the date when it was published, updated, or stated. The citation should also include the name of the **source** in order to make clear to the audience that the source is credible. This should be the name of the journal or periodical in which the information appears, the sponsoring organization of the website or study, the name of the person you are quoting and his/her credentials, or the author's name and title of a book. Remember, you need to report the information about the source that informs the audience that this source is credible. Thus, use the journal name rather than the name of the author when citing this information. Review the information below in regards to what should be cited.

TYPE OF SOURCE	WHAT TO CITE, VERBALLY	EXAMPLE
Journal	Name of publication	*Communication Education*
Periodical	Name of publication	*Scientific American*
Book	Primary author's name and title of book	Henry Kissinger *World Order*
Interview	Name of person and credentials	Dr. John Scheb UT Professor of Political Science
Website	Sponsoring organization	NASA

Citing information from a journal article or periodical

When citing information from a journal article you should include the name of the journal and the date it was published. Occasionally, it will be useful to your audience to include the author's name. However, in most cases, the name of the journal assigns more credibility to the information than an author's name with which no one is familiar. Avoid the use of words such as "prove" when reporting information from journals. Rather, make use of words such as the study "suggests," "finds," or "offers evidence" to support a specific point.

Citing statistics

When reporting statistical information, whether from a journal or a sponsoring organization, avoid the use of words such as "prove." Instead, as stated previously, state that the statistics "suggest" or "support." By their nature, statistics are not designed to prove. Rather, they are designed to suggest or support conclusions. You must also cite the date the article was published. Adhere to the following guidelines when using statistics in your speech:

- Use statistics when you need to quantify ideas. Do not use words such as "many," "a lot," or "often."

- Use statistics sparingly.

- Round complicated numbers (e.g., if a study finds that 5,972 people have experienced a particular event, round this number to "almost 6,000 people").

- Explain your statistics in terms of percentages or fractions.

Citing information from books

The criteria for citing a book is a bit different. Since you do not have a name of a journal or periodical to cite, you must rely on the title. When you state the title, you should also include the primary author's name. Also, cite the date the book was published.

Citing information from websites

When citing information from a website include the author's name and credentials (researcher, college professor, etc.) OR the sponsoring organization. You should also include the date the article was published or when it was posted on the Web. If the author's name or sponsoring organization are not available, do not use the website.

Citing testimony from personal interview

When conducting an interview, include the name of the person you interviewed, their expertise or experience with the topic (their credentials), and the date you conducted the interview. You should also note that you were the interviewer.

Additional tips for citing information

You will notice in the examples of citations above that the following suggestions will help your verbal citations flow when citing information in your speech.

- **Cite before stating the information.** You will find that it is more useful for your audience to give the source and date before the supporting information in the citation. This way, your audience knows that it is credible and current before hearing the information.

- **Vary the way that you introduce the source.** There are many other options to introduce your citations without always using "according to."

- **Do not use secondary sources.** A secondary source occurs when a speaker cites a source that is found within another source. For example, if the author of a book you are reading describes the words or ideas of another person, avoid using this secondhand account of what was said. The author of the book you are reading may have taken the ideas of the other person out of context or misinterpreted their meaning. When you encounter this type of situation, try to obtain the original source—do not rely on the secondary source to be accurate. If the original is simply not available, cite the source that you tangibly have but make clear that this is a secondary citation.

THREE-STEP PROCESS TO CITE SUPPORTING MATERIAL

In order to maximize the impact of your outside research on your audience, you will need to employ the following three-step process when citing supporting material.

1. **Preview the evidence**. Begin by introducing your audience to what is coming next so that they are prepared to hear the evidence.

   - "Automobiles are more fuel efficient than ever."

2. **Cite the evidence**. This is where you will "plug in" your citation.

   - "According to the latest 2013 report from the National Transportation Board, average automobile fuel efficiency has reached 30 miles per gallon."

3. **Explain the evidence**. After your citation, do not just move on. Take the time to interpret the evidence for the listeners. Specifically, seek to manage how audience members draw conclusions.

   - "Most of us are far more fuel conscious when purchasing a car today and that concern for fuel efficiency will continue to grow in the future."

APA Tutorial

In this course you will be expected to follow APA format for citing sources. Below are common examples of appropriate citations for various types of sources to assist you with the list of References at the end of your preparation outline. In addition to the criteria for specific sources, follow the guidelines listed below for creating a reference page.

- All citations listed should be in alphabetical order by the primary author's last name or the name of the sponsoring organization.

- The name of the publication (journal or periodical) as well as a book title should be italicized.

- Each line of the citation after the first should be indented as shown.

- Each word in the title of the article should be lowercase, except for the first word in the title.

JOURNAL ARTICLE

Morton, J., & O'Brien, D. (2005). Selling your design: Oral communication pedagogy in design education. *Communication Education, 54,* 6–19.

Note: Authors, year, title of article, title of journal, volume number, page numbers

---

JOURNAL ARTICLE FROM DATABASE

Hahn, D., & Homan, T. (2000). A closer look at the drug abuse-maternal aggression link. *Journal of Interpersonal Violence, 15,* 503–522. Retrieved May 20, 2005, from ProQuest database.

JOURNAL ARTICLE, INTERNET-ONLY JOURNAL
Bergen, D. (2002, Spring). The role of pretend play in children's cognitive development. *Early Childhood Research & Practice, 4* (1). Retrieved February 1, 2005, from http://ecrp.uiuc.edu/v4n1/bergen.html

BOOK
Deetz, S. A. (1992). *Democracy in the age of corporate colonization: Developments in communication and the politics of everyday life.* Albany: State University of New York Press.

CHAPTER IN AN EDITED BOOK
Shea, J. D. (1992). Personality and interpersonal communication. In M. L. Knapp (Ed.), *Religion and mental health* (pp. 70–84). New York: Oxford University Press.

STAND-ALONE WEB DOCUMENT (NO DATE)
Barnes, M. E. (n.d.). *Notable people in psychology of religion.* Retrieved August 3, 2005, from http://www.psywww.com/psyrelig/psyrelpr.htm

STAND-ALONE WEB DOCUMENT (NO AUTHOR, NO DATE)
Trinity University. (n.d.). *Gender and society*. Retrieved December 3, 2004, from http://www.trinity.edu/~mkearl/gender.html

Note: Sponsoring organization, no date, title of document, date retrieved, exact link

MAGAZINE
Able, F.A., & Squire, L.R. (2005, September 10). Breaking down scientific barriers to the study of communication. *Science, 29*, 113–120.

NEWSPAPER
Smith, J. (2005, September 30). Health costs affect economic, social status. *The News Chronicle Bulletin*, p.3.

BROCHURE/PAMPHLET
Center for Advanced Communication Studies (2006). *Guidelines for interpreting communication research* [Brochure]. Louisville, KY: Author.

INTERVIEW
Harden, E. (2005, October 5). Personal communication.

Note: Name of person who was interviewed, date interview was conducted

CLASS SURVEY

Bailey, C. (2005, September 26). Public Speaking Class. Personal Communication.

Note: Current APA guidelines do not require the citation of interviews or other personal communication. However, for the purposes of this course we do require that you cite personal communication, if that source is used in your speech.

ENCYCLOPEDIA ENTRY

Bormann, W. (2004). Human development. *The new encyclopedia* (Vol. 28, pp. 423–432). Chicago: Holt Press.

MOTION PICTURE

Bates, M. (Producer), & Lonergan, K. (Writer/Director). (2001). *Count on us* [Motion picture]. United States: Acme Pictures.

TELEVISION BROADCAST

Bartlett, J. (Executive Producer). (2005, October 17). *The WKZZ Nightly News* [Television broadcast]. Knoxville, TN: Mountain Broadcasting Service.

Key Terms/Concepts to Know

Source criteria	Evaluating sources
Credible sources	Scholarly
Current sources	Peer review
Types of sources	Popular press
Scholarly sources	Choosing supporting material
Peer review	Facts
Web-based sources	Statistics
Citation database	Expert testimony
Reference sources	Peer testimony
	Examples
	Stories

ORGANIZING AND OUTLINING YOUR SPEECH

CHAPTER OBJECTIVES

This chapter is designed to help you understand:

- How to organize your speech

- How to identify main points

- How to use parallel structure

- How to use organizational patterns

- How to develop a preparation outline

- How to develop a speaking outline

Photo provided by John William Haas

In general, structured messages are more effective than unstructured messages. Without a structured message, if you achieve your goals it is by chance, not by design. Effective speakers do not rely on chance to achieve their goals. Moreover, without organizing the information in some fashion, the speech will appear as a lengthy stream of consciousness. Not surprisingly, there is little hope of an audience following seemingly unrelated ideas in a speech. Many speakers think that their speech is organized, since in their mind, the message is clear. However, without using the guidelines reviewed in this chapter, the information will not come across in an organized way to the audience. The structure and organization of your speech will affect:

- How easy it is to **follow** the speech;

- How **clear** the information will be to the audience;

- How **competent** the audience views you as a speaker; and

- How **confident** you feel about your preparation and delivery.

In this chapter we will examine the key elements of speech organization and structure. As you read the material keep in mind that you will be expected to deliver a structured, organized speech, and that this step in the speech-making process will almost certainly require the most amount of time in your speech preparation.

Main Points

After you complete the majority of your research, the next step is to identify the main points of the speech. Main points categorize the information in the body of your speech. The main points will emerge from the research that you conduct. That is, as you gather information, you should begin to see how this body of information can be separated into broad categories. However, until you gather information to support your purpose, it will be difficult or impossible to develop main points for a speech. Keep in mind—the main points are the key informational items that will allow you to achieve the specific purpose.

All of your main points should be developed based on the specific purpose. Consider the following example.

To inform my audience about the three most common types of computer operating systems for personal computers.

INCORRECT MAIN POINTS	CORRECT MAIN POINTS
I. Microsoft Windows	I. Microsoft Windows
II. Mac OS X	II. Mac OS X
III. Linux	III. Linux
IV. Purchasing decisions	

In the example above, content can be added as a sub-point to each main point later, but the main points should stand alone as key concepts in support of your objective. Main points should be tied directly to the specific purpose.

After you have completed the majority of your research and developed the main points, you must decide how to state the main points. The guidelines below will assist you in this task.

NUMBER OF MAIN POINTS

Your major speaking assignments this term (the informative and persuasive speeches) will involve two to five main points. If you have developed more than five main points for the major speech assignments, you are seeking to accomplish too much in the time available. Keep in mind the time allotted for presentations in this course will limit you to no more than five main points.

You should also seek to separate or combine main points effectively. Each main point should focus on a single idea. If you find completely different information within a single main point, divide the information into separate main points. In contrast, if you have two main points that include very similar information, combine them to represent one general point.

WORDING AND PARALLEL LANGUAGE

State the main points in similar fashion. That is, use consistent or parallel language to develop main points. For example, in Martin Luther King, Jr.'s "I Have a Dream" speech, he made very effective use of parallel structure. Parallel structure unifies the ideas in the main point around the purpose of the speech.

Using parallel language structure allowed Dr. King to underscore key ideas or main points with impactful imagery. Moreover, Dr. King did not limit his use of parallel language to main points. For each subpoint within a main point, he made effective use of parallel language that created smooth movement from one idea to the next. While Dr. King was a truly gifted orator, you can also use this same kind of organizational pattern to make your speech memorable and effective. In addition to adding a unifying function and impactful imagery, main points also perform other functions.

In a sense, the main points function as road signs. When these are apparent to the audience, they have a clear road to follow. Without these road signs, it is difficult for the audience to know where they are going. You have a better chance of making the speech memorable and achieving your goals if the audience remembers and sees unity in the main points of the speech. It will be difficult for your audience to pick out your main points and follow the speech if you do not word main points in a similar fashion as represented in the example below:

- **Specific Purpose**: To inform my audience of the three major ways the University of Tennessee is advancing to Top 25 status.

- **Central Idea**: The three major ways that the University is advancing to Top 25 status is by renovating campus facilities, recruiting high caliber students, and increasing financial support from alumni.

- **Main Points:**

  I.   The University of Tennessee is advancing to Top 25 status by renovating campus facilities.

  II. The University of Tennessee is advancing to Top 25 status by recruiting high caliber students.

  III. The University of Tennessee is advancing to Top 25 status by increasing financial support from alumni.

Did you notice that the main points are similarly worded in the central idea? Moreover, did you notice the parallel construction with specific kinds of words? In this case, if you begin one main point with an action verb that ends with "ing" (in this case, advancing), begin the next main point with the same action verb (in this case, advancing).

I have a dream that one day this nation *will* rise up and live out the true meaning of its creed: "We hold these truths to be self-evident, that all men are created equal."

I have a dream that one day on the red hills of Georgia, the sons of former slaves and the sons of former slave owners *will be* able to sit down together at the table of brotherhood.

—Martin Luther King, Jr.

LENGTH

Seek to devote approximately equal amounts of time to each main point. It is unrealistic to expect that you can devote exactly the same amount of time to each main point, but you should seek to balance the amount of time devoted to each main point as evenly as possible. If the time devoted to one main point is significantly different from the time devoted to others, you should reconsider the number of main points that you plan to use for the speech. If you encounter this situation, you may need to combine similar main points or delete the information from the speech. When speakers devote unequal time to main points, it is often the case that the speaker views the worth of the main points in the speech differently. As speakers, we tend to spend more time on the most important items and less time on information that is not as important. If that is the case, consider whether less important information can be deleted from the speech or incorporated into more "important" main points.

ARRANGEMENT

Arrangement addresses the question of how you order the information you plan to present. To begin, you should select the arrangement (organizational pattern) that best allows you to achieve your objective. Thus, always think strategically when you order the main points.

We will share with you five different kinds of organizational patterns. These patterns include chronological, spatial, topical, cause and effect, and problem–solution. Below you will find information about these organizational patterns and how they are tied to the central idea of a speech.

Organizational Patterns

After you have followed the previous guidelines for constructing main points, begin assembling the specific purpose and central idea around one organizational pattern. As noted, select the organizational pattern that is best suited to achieving your objectives. There are five types of organization patterns to choose from to order your main points but some may be better able to assist you in achieving your objectives in an informative speech while others may be better able to assist you to achieve your objectives in a persuasive speech. Informative speeches are often (but not always!) associated with chronological, spatial, and topical patterns of organizing. Persuasive speeches are often (but not always!) associated with cause and effect and problem–solution patterns of organizing. You will decide which organizational pattern to use based on your specific purpose and the type of speech.

CHRONOLOGICAL

This pattern organizes your speech in terms of time. It is used most often with informative speeches involving processes or events since its sequential steps or stages spotlight movement through time.

- Specific Purpose: To inform my audience about the four steps in group decision making.

- Central Idea: The four major steps of group decision making include orientation, conflict, emergence, and reinforcement.

SPATIAL

This pattern is often used for informative speeches that involve portions of a whole, tangible object (e.g., the regions of a country, the sections of a large building, or the sections of a plane). It will divide the object into sections for discussion on the basis of space. That is, the main points can be discussed from top to bottom, left to right, or west to east.

- Specific Purpose: To inform my audience about the five major regions of the United States.

- Central Idea: The five major regions of the United States include the Northeast, Southeast, Midwest, Southwest, and West.

TOPICAL

A topical pattern is often used because of its adaptability to many types of topics and purposes. Many informative speeches, as well as persuasive speeches on questions of fact or value, call for topical order.

- Specific Purpose: To inform my audience about the three key factors that determine career success.

- Central Idea: The three key factors that influence career success include effective oral communication skills, effective written communication skills, and motivation.

CAUSE AND EFFECT

This pattern indicates a cause–effect relationship exists between the two main points. Cause is understood as why something happens; effect is understood as what happens. For example, if the cause is rainfall, the effect is plant growth. Keep in mind when using this pattern that there are often multiple causes for any particular effect. For example, rainfall is a cause for plant growth. But, so is fertilizer. Since there may be many different causes for any single effect, speakers make use of two different ways to organize a cause and effect pattern.

There are two ways in which cause and effect patterns can be organized. The first option organizes the information so that each point stated as a cause is followed immediately by the effect(s). The first option is used when the effects are different for each cause. The second option organizes the information so that the first main point addresses all of the major cause(s) and is followed by the second main point that lays out the major effect(s).

Option One

- Specific Purpose: To inform my audience of the three major causes of obesity.

- Central Idea: The three major causes of obesity are lack of exercise, nutrition, and genetics.

Option Two

- Specific Purpose: To inform my audience of the two major reasons why people abuse drugs.

- Central Idea: The two major causes of drug abuse are to feel good or to feel better.

PROBLEM–SOLUTION

This pattern divides the information presented in the speech into two main points—a main point that identifies the problem(s) and a main point that identifies the solution. This pattern is most often used for persuasive speeches since it is well-suited to persuade an audience to support a particular course of action. By establishing a problem exists, a speaker compels the audience to consider a change in attitudes and behavior.

The most effective use of this pattern is associated with a single solution. That is, do not provide the audience with multiple ways of addressing the problem(s). Rather, the speaker should focus on a single solution. The only reason to discuss other ways of resolving the problem(s) would be to make clear that the solution you offer is superior to other possible solutions.

- Specific Purpose: To persuade my audience to use public forms of transportation.

- Central Idea: Private transportation is causing problems that can be overcome through the use of public transportation.

Placing Supporting Material

Supporting material provides evidence or "backs up" the ideas for your main points. The supporting material is useful to listeners in order to determine whether to accept the message. All supporting materials should be directly relevant to the main points they support.

After the supporting materials are gathered, you are ready to organize the speech by:

- Choosing/wording the main points;

- Writing your central idea; and

- Grouping material under the appropriate main point in outline form.

The supporting material will become **sub-points** in the speech that serve as evidence to "back up" the main points. The following is a guide to help you organize this information quickly and effectively.

> *Sometimes a concept is baffling not because it is profound but because it is wrong.*
>
> —Edward O. Wilson

GUIDE TO ORGANIZING INFORMATION

1. Print all of the sources you have found in order to pull together all of the information that has been gathered.

2. Assign a number to each separate source.

3. Write out the main points in outline form.

4. Gather several different colored highlighters and assign a color to each main point.

5. Start with the first source and highlight everything that supports the first main point.

6. Follow this procedure for every source using a different color highlighter for each source.

7. Once you have highlighted the information in each source, insert the information into your outline under each main point that it represents.

8. As you transfer information, do not forget to note the source (you will need this information to cite your sources).

9. Once in this visual outline format you can begin to edit the information that may be redundant or not needed.

10. At this point, consider paraphrasing information to make it clearer to your audience and to help you feel comfortable with the words that are used in the speech.

11. Construct a reference page following APA format that lists the articles cited.

Connectives

Connectives are among the most important components to effective speech organization. Connectives are words or phrases that tie one thought to another and indicate the relationship between them. They promote a unified, coherent speech. Several different kinds of connectives can be used to help you deliver an effective speech. On the following page you will find a set of tables that provide specific examples of connective words and phrases. The tables are followed by a description of the different kinds of connectives you will use in a speech.

CONNECTIVES INVOLVING TIME

First (second, third, etc.)	Finally	Next
When	Last	Until then
At this point	Meanwhile	Next time
Since	Before that	In the end
Afterwards	On another occasion	While
Previously	Later on	At once
At this moment	In the future	In the past
In the beginning	Now	

CONNECTIVES INVOLVING SIMILARITY OR ADDING A POINT

In addition	Moreover	Not only
Furthermore	As well	Also
Not only	Interestingly	Additionally

CONNECTIVES INVOLVING DIFFERENCES OR OPPOSITION TO A POINT

However	In contrast	Instead
Alternatively	On the contrary	In spite of this
On the other hand	In fact	Differs from
Nevertheless	But	In other respects

CONNECTIVES INVOLVING EXPLANATION

For example	For instance	In other words
That is to say	To clarify	To repeat

CONNECTIVES INVOLVING LISTS

First (second, third, etc.)	Next	In the first place
To begin	To conclude	In sum

TRANSITIONS

A transition is a full sentence used between main points in the body of a speech. Transitions tell the audience where you have been and where you are going. This reminds the audience of your last main point and previews your next main point. Transitions are the most important of all of the connectives because they help your audience pick out the main points of the speech. You will notice that a full transition includes both an internal preview and internal summary (discussed below). Make sure that you are using full transitions between main points in the body of your speech. In essence, a transition consists of three components: the main point that was just discussed, the main point you will discuss next, and the purpose of your speech. You must use a transition between each main point.

- "Now that we have covered the problems associated with private cars, let's discuss the benefits that public transportation can bring to all of us."

INTERNAL PREVIEWS

Internal previews are used to explain to the audience what will be covered next in your speech. The main internal preview that you will use in your speech is between the introduction and body. The central idea, discussed at the end of your introduction, is not considered an internal preview. An internal preview, like the one below, should come after your central idea (main points) to identify the first main point to be covered. Notice that the internal preview below includes a list-related signpost. The type of connective is identified by the entire phrase or sentence.

- "First, I will talk about the traffic congestion caused by private transportation."

INTERNAL SUMMARIES

These are the opposite of internal previews and are used only to recap for your audience what you have covered. The main internal summary will be at the beginning of your conclusion before you recap the main points. This signals to the audience that you have come to the conclusion.

- "In summary, I hope this speech has given you a better understanding of the problems associated with private transportation and the benefits associated with public transportation."

SIGNPOSTS

While all of the other types of connectives tell the audience where the speech has been, is going, or both, signposts are shorter words or phrases that tell your audience where you are currently in the speech. These should be used throughout the body of the speech at the beginning of sub-points. Your information does not have to be chronological for you to use signposts. You are using them to identify the order of your information.

- Some examples of signposts are "first," "second," "third," "next," "last," "then," and "in addition."

In order for connectives to be effective, the main points must be worded in the same fashion throughout the presentation. Even minor word changes will confuse the audience.

Writing the Introduction and Conclusion

After you have completed the body of the speech in outline form, you are ready to add the introduction and conclusion. There are certain components that are expected to be included in both the introduction and conclusion in the order that is described below. Research suggests that the first item (primacy effect) and last item (recency effect) heard by an audience tends to be remembered most readily. Since these effects impact the introduction and conclusion, it is important to construct these portions of the speech carefully.

INTRODUCTION COMPONENTS

The introduction to a speech can serve several different functions. For the purposes of this course, we will focus on the following four major components for the speech introduction.

Attention-gaining Device

When you begin your speech you must first gain the attention and interest of the audience. **Do not begin your speech with your name and/or your topic**. Rather, choose from any of the following methods of gaining attention. Choose only one method and keep it brief. Depending on which method you choose, this task can be accomplished in one sentence.

- Create a hypothetical example. This is probably the most effective way to gain the attention of the audience because it is the most relevant. If you create a situation in which they can see themselves or identify with on a personal level it will gain their attention. For example, if your speech is about your distracted driving, you may want to begin with "Imagine that you are standing on the side of the road waiting for the police to arrive. You struck a tree while texting and totaled your parent's car. How will you break the news to your parents?"

- State a startling statistic. This can convey the importance of the topic by quantifying the idea. It would tell the audience how often something occurs or how many people do or believe something and make them curious to hear the topic. This is effective when you have novel information or a more unfamiliar topic. For example, "If current trends continue, the population of the United States will increase to over 600 million in 2080, and in 2150 will be equal to the population of China."

- Ask a question of the audience. If asking your audience a question, make it clear to them whether or not you want a response by saying something to the effect of "By a show of hands, how many of you plan to vote in the upcoming election?" then wait for a response. If you do not require a response just ask your audience to think about their personal response. A word of caution about using questions: How will it impact your speech if audience members respond in a way that you do not anticipate? In addition, do not ask a question when the answer is obviously known to the audience. For example, "Do you use light bulbs?" The answer is an obvious yes and is not likely to hold the attention of the audience.

- Begin with a quote. When quoting someone, make sure that you are conversational so that the first item in your speech is not being read. It is important to begin with a high level of eye contact in order to gain the attention of the audience. For example, "Strive not to be a success, but rather to be of value." This quote from Albert Einstein captures a theme that could be used throughout the speech. Moreover, it offers great potential if used in parallel structure.

- Tell a story. You can choose to begin with a story, but you must prepare the story in advance, and keep it **brief**. If not worked out in advance, the delivery of the story will likely be longer and less well organized than you anticipated. This is not the kind of first impression a speaker should create. You may choose to only tell part of a story to gain attention in your introduction so your audience will continue to listen to find out what happens later in your speech.

Purpose

After you gain the attention of your audience, you must state clearly the purpose of your speech to avoid confusing the audience. This is when and where your topic is revealed to the audience. Even if the audience already knows the topic, a speaker should restate it during the introduction. You should take the information from your specific purpose to do this, but do not say, "My purpose is to inform my audience about…" You should be conversational and talk to them, not about them. This can be accomplished in one sentence. For example, "I'm here today to tell you about the three major causes of obesity in children."

- **Define major terms**. You should also use this step to define any major terms that you will be using throughout your entire speech and are crucial to your audience's understanding of your purpose. Not every speech will require you to include this. If you will only be using certain unfamiliar or technical terms or acronyms during one part of the body of the speech then wait to define them there. However, if you are relying on the term in your purpose or throughout the speech, include the meaning here.

- **Relevance statement**. Seek to relate to your specific audience in the introduction of the speech. This is where you will link the topic with the audience. Tell your listeners, in concrete terms, why they need to learn this information or why this should be important to them. Simply put, make the topic relevant to your audience. This outwardly conveys why the audience should listen and why they need to know this information. This statement should also appear on your informative topic sheet before submission.

CHAPTER 9

Photo provided by John William Haas

Sometimes, speakers are able to relate the topic well enough to the audience by using a creative attention-gaining device. However, if relevance was not clearly established by the attention-gaining device, you will need to include a separate relevance statement in this step. For example, if you use a hypothetical example as your attention-gaining device to get your audience thinking about themselves, you would not need to do this again.

Credibility

After gaining the attention of the audience and revealing your purpose, you must establish your credibility as the speaker. That is, tell the audience what connects you with the topic. Credibility, in this case, is telling your audience why you chose the topic. This is a matter of being perceived by the audience as qualified to speak on a particular topic or being competent. You may hold a certain level of knowledge or possess a keen interest or be passionate about the topic. You may have experience doing it or someone in your family or a friend may have experienced it. This will also better allow you to use your personal experience later in the speech. Whatever the case, be honest about why you chose the topic. This can be accomplished in one sentence.

Central Idea

The last component of the introduction will be the central idea. As you recall, the central idea previews the body of the speech by sharing with the audience your main points. This statement tells an audience what to listen for in the rest of the speech. Because it is found at the end of the introduction, the central idea provides a smooth lead-in to the internal preview and the body of the speech.

Below is a sample introduction for the preparation outline:

Introduction

I. Attention-gaining device

II. Specific purpose (be conversational)

    A. Define major terms from purpose (if necessary)

    B. Relevance statement (why your audience needs to know this)

III. Credibility (why you chose the topic)

IV. Central idea

INTRODUCTION GUIDELINES

While it is clear that speakers seek to achieve certain objectives with the speech introduction, not every introduction is equally effective. When preparing your introduction, use the following guidelines for developing your message.

- **Do develop the introduction after the body of the speech is complete.** As stated previously, the body of the speech needs to be complete before you add the introduction. The introduction should not drive the decision about what to include in the body of the speech.

- **Do include the four major introduction objectives.** Review the introduction to determine if all of the four major components appear.

- **Do be brief.** For a speech that is four to seven minutes in length, your introduction should be approximately 45–50 seconds. Depending on what you choose for your attention-gaining device and if any terms are defined, your introduction may be closer to one minute. All you need to do is cover what is discussed above and no more. Since each of the four components to the introduction could be delivered in a total of four sentences, you have the opportunity to keep the introduction brief.

- **Do be creative with the introduction.** Come up with material that creates the largest impact on your audience. Be creative with what you choose and construct to make your first impression.

CONCLUSION COMPONENTS

Consistent with the introduction, the conclusion also serves a number of important functions. Conclusions should include the following components:

Internal Summary

An internal summary at the beginning of the conclusion will signal to the audience that you are in the process of concluding the speech. Letting your audience know that you have arrived at the conclusion fulfills an important function. Abrupt endings leave listeners surprised and unfulfilled. If you do not begin your conclusion with a statement such as "In summary" or some other internal summary, your audience may not know where you are in your speech.

Immediately after you signal the end of your speech with an internal summary, summarize the main points. You should seek to reinforce the audience's understanding of and commitment to the central idea of the speech. In order to do this, you will be expected to recap your main points for the audience. As you can see in the example below, this task can be accomplished in a single sentence.

- "To recap, I hope that you now have a better understanding of the three major causes of heart disease which include smoking, a sedentary lifestyle, and genetic predisposition."

Final Statement

Just as the attention-gaining device was the first element of your speech, your final statement is the last element of your speech and what your audience is most likely to remember. Ask yourself what you want the audience to take away from the speech. This statement should be concise, dramatic, and memorable. You may choose to end with a quotation that encompasses this, or a powerful statement of your own. To create greater unity in your speech, you may choose to refer back to the introduction of the speech using parallel language.

CONCLUSION GUIDELINES

As with introductions, not all conclusions are equally effective. Speakers will more likely succeed in developing effective conclusions based on the following criteria:

- **Do develop the conclusion after the body of the speech has been developed.** The body and introduction of your speech should be complete before you add the conclusion.

- **Do be brief.** For a speech that is four to seven minutes, the conclusion should be no more than 25–35 seconds long.

- **Do conclude with a bang.** Your conclusion should bring the ideas in your speech to a peak. This is the final thought the audience will be left with, and you want the audience to remember an effective, strong ending.

Outlining the Speech

THE PREPARATION OUTLINE

Outlining the speech is important in the organization of the material. Speakers use an outline to help them think through the various stages of the speech. An outline is a kind of visual scheme of the organization of your speech. It identifies the main arguments for your speech objective as well as the subtopics that will be covered for each main point. Outlines range from an informal use of indenting and graphics to a formal use of Roman numerals and letters. Regardless of the degree of formality, however, the function of an outline is to help you consider the most effective way to say what you want to say.

When preparing the speech outline, you will not write it in narrative form as you would a paper. Instead, you will categorize the information in the body of your speech into levels that include the main points and sub-points. The preparation outline is the full representation of the entire speech that you will create as you prepare the informative and persuasive speeches.

THE SPEAKING OUTLINE

The speaking outline will serve as your notes during the speech. When you have completed the preparation outline, transfer the most important parts of the speech to a speaking outline format prior to practicing the speech. You should use note cards for the speaking outline rather than sheets of paper. Do not use the preparation outline for notes—it includes too much information for you to use appropriately.

There are several different ways you can develop a speaking outline. The following guidelines should be helpful in the creation of the speaking outline.

- **Do use the same format as the preparation outline.** This format will provide enough structure in a visual framework that you can easily follow when delivering the speech.

- **Do use phrases.** The speaking outline is much more concise than a preparation outline. The major reason for this is to take away the temptation to read or memorize your speech rather than delivering the speech extemporaneously. Do not write complete sentences in the speaking outline. Instead, use only words or phrases (bullets) that will trigger your memory about what you want to say. From this phrase or word outline, you will be able to make greater use of your own words and deliver the speech in a conversational manner.

- **Do make the preparation outline legible.** Your eyes will need to be able to fall on your speaking outline during the speech and locate where you are in the speech. You will not be able to locate information on the speaking outline if you do not print it legibly or if you print it too small. So, print neatly using large letters!

- **Do include delivery cues.** After you complete the majority of your speaking outline, go back and include reminders for yourself at specific times during the speech. In some cases, you may need to write in the margin of your notes delivery components that you should concentrate on during your speech. For example, if you know that you need to improve by projecting your voice more fully, then note that throughout your speech as a reminder. In addition, you may also need to include visual aid cues to help you remember when to show something to the audience. The rule of thumb when preparing a speaking outline is to include what you need to deliver the speech effectively.

Key Terms/Concepts to Know

Main points	Placing supporting material
Parallel language/parallel structure	Connectives
Specific purpose	Transitions
Central idea	Internal previews
Organizational patterns	Internal summaries
Chronological	Signposts
Spatial	Introductions
Topical	Conclusions
Cause and effect	Preparation outline
Problem–solution	Speaking outline

CHAPTER 9

STUDENT NOTES

USING LANGUAGE

CHAPTER OBJECTIVES

This chapter is designed to help you understand:

- How to use and evaluate language in public speaking

- How communication rules effect speeches

- How we assign meanings to words

- How to sort out appropriate language use and inappropriate use

- How to use vivid language

Language may be viewed as a resource that public speakers use to convey ideas. Regrettably, not every person is equally skillful in the use of language. Our goal for this chapter is to advance your understanding of the role of language in public speaking situations. Armed with this knowledge, you will be able to develop speeches with vivid, descriptive language.

Language and Public Speaking

In a sense, speakers work with a "set of tools" to achieve their objectives. The set of tools that you will use to "construct" a speech include voice quality, body movement, supporting information, the pattern of organizing, and the visual aids that you will use for the speech. All of these items are used by the speaker to achieve his/her objectives. Moreover, the speaker can polish his/her skills with each of these elements. A very important instrument in the speaker's toolbox involves language.

Photo provided by John William Haas

Language may be thought of as a symbol system through which we create and exchange meanings. Language use is governed by a set of rules that speakers are expected to follow. For example, we have rules about how people are expected to initiate conversations as well as how people should conclude conversations. We have rules that involve turn-taking in conversations. Quite literally, there are hundreds of rules that govern the way we use language.

Language Rules

The rules for language use are prescriptive. That is, the rules lay out for us what we are expected to do when we use language. The rules for public speaking situations vary a bit from the rules that govern language use in conversations. For example, our day-to-day conversations are governed by turn-taking rules. It is a violation of language rules for one person to do all the talking while others do all of the listening. Consider how you would respond to a situation in a face-to-face setting in which the other party did all of the talking. For most of us, we would begin to find ways of letting the other party know that we expect our turn to speak.

In public speaking situations, that rule for turn-taking is different. In this situation we expect one party to do most all of the talking and all others are expected to do most of the listening. While a vast number of rules exist that govern our use of language, we will focus our attention on four rules or maxims that you will be expected to follow.

CLARITY

The clarity rule suggests that speakers should avoid ambiguity. That is, a speaker should not use language that is vague or unclear when communicating with others. Use terminology that your specific audience will understand. While being professional and adapting to your audience, be sure to use terms that you feel comfortable using.

RELATION

The relation rule suggests that speakers should make clear the connections between their ideas. Use language that directly makes the connection. This can be accomplished through explanation or through comparison. Seek to manage how the audience understands the relationships between your ideas. Connectives provide a powerful tool for making explicit how ideas are related.

QUALITY

The quality rule suggests that we should tell the truth as we know it. You can do this by reporting your information accurately as you find it. In addition, do not paraphrase others' ideas to such an extent that the information no longer resembles the original information.

QUANTITY

The quantity rule suggests that speakers should say no more and no less than what is needed to convey a message. How do audience members communicate to speakers that the quantity rule is being violated? In too many cases, a speaker will use four or five sentences to say what he or she could have stated in one sentence. The way to condense the material in your speech is to continue to ask yourself while preparing the outline how the information you plan to discuss will directly help you achieve your speaking goal(s). If you can't tie the information directly to achieving the speaking goal(s), eliminate the information.

Clearly, there are times when we violate the language rules that speakers are expected to follow. For example, when trying to persuade an audience that is hostile to your purpose, it makes sense to defer your purpose statement until late in the speech. In this situation, you would violate the rule on clearness. Audience members will judge your performance, in part, on the extent to which you conform to the rules for public speaking. Consider carefully any decision to violate the rules.

Language is a very powerful tool that allows speakers to convey meanings to listeners. Since language involves a system of symbols, speakers must be cautious about the meanings that receivers assign to symbols. Simply put, a **symbol** may be thought of as one thing standing for something else. The wildly popular use of :) in e-mail messages symbolizes or stands for a smiling face. However, it might be interpreted as meaning agreement, I am happy, I am happy with you, and so on. Since the meanings we assign to symbols are not always clear-cut, public speakers must consider how audience members are likely to understand and interpret the symbols (verbal and nonverbal messages, visual aids, and so on) used in the speech.

Language and Meaning

Language is used by speakers to define the situation. That is, speakers use messages to shape the way listeners come to understand what is going on around them. For example, does this situation present us with an opportunity or a problem? Does this situation involve work, or should it be understood as play? Not surprisingly, receivers do not always accept how speakers define the situation through their language use. However, skillful language use does provide the speaker with a powerful tool to shape the way listeners view the world around them. When interpreting messages, receivers employ the following meanings of language:

DENOTATIVE MEANINGS

Denotative meanings involve the literal meaning or dictionary definition of a word or phrase. Thus, the denotative meaning of the word "cool" to a receiver involves chilly temperatures.

CONNOTATIVE MEANINGS

The connotative meaning of a word or phrase is more subjective. Connotative meanings extend beyond the literal meaning of a word and are subject to interpretation by speakers and listeners. It usually evokes some sort of emotion in the listener. For example, the connotative meaning of "cool" may be that an individual or event is viewed positively. However, if the speaker uses the word "cool" in sarcastic

CHAPTER 10

fashion, it may mean that the individual or event is viewed negatively. As a speaker, it is important to recognize that the members of your audience may vary in the connotative meanings that they assign to your message.

Appropriate Use of Language

Since we know that receivers place different meanings to our language, keep in mind the following tips concerning language when preparing and delivering speeches:

BE CLEAR

If the audience is uncertain as to the meaning of your message, you will not achieve your objectives. Do not "beat around the bush"; instead come out and say what you mean to avoid confusion.

BE ACCURATE

Inaccurate messages will diminish your credibility in the eyes of the receivers. If you paraphrase information, make sure that the meaning does not change.

BE MEMORABLE

Use language in such a way that your message is unforgettable. You can achieve the goal of creating memorable messages by using language to bring issues into sharp focus or bringing together ideas in a novel way. For example, the message, "Ask not what your country can do for you, ask what you can do for your country" created a lasting memory for listeners because two different ideas were brought together in a novel way.

BE CREATIVE

Use creative, vivid words and phrases to generate and maintain interest in the message. Avoid the trite phrases that we hear every day. For the amount of information that you will include from others, make sure that you also create your own expressions to gain more credibility.

Inappropriate Use of Language

When preparing and delivering speeches, avoid the following types of language:

BIASED LANGUAGE

Language that reflects a bias against or toward individuals on the basis of gender, race, religion, background, or group membership is unacceptable. In fact, according to the credo used in this course, it is unethical.

CULTURALLY INSENSITIVE LANGUAGE

Language that is not sensitive to cultural differences is unacceptable. Even if something does not seem offensive to you, it does not mean that it will not offend members of your audience. According to the credo used in this course, it is unethical. When used, it damages your credibility as a speaker.

CLICHÉS

Such overused expressions as "it is what it is" are to be avoided in speeches because they do not add much to the message or suggest original thinking on the part of the speaker. Information that is tired will not capture the attention of the audience. Consider the following: Do you know someone who uses too many clichés on a regular basis? Do you enjoy talking with that person?

Vivid Language

One way to make your message pleasant to listen to and memorable is to make use of vivid language. Vivid language produces distinct mental images in the receivers and holds their attention. With the language that you select for your speech, you paint a picture for the audience. The "picture" is most readily understood by receivers when the speaker uses:

CONCRETE VS. ABSTRACT WORDS

Concrete language enables the audience to create a mental picture of a real, tangible item creating **imagery**. For example, the University of Tennessee is concrete; school is abstract. As discussed before, you want to avoid being abstract unless you have a sound reason (will this help me achieve my objective?).

DESCRIPTIVE LANGUAGE

Descriptive language adds detail to the mental image in the mind of the receiver. Simply put, descriptive language involves the use of adjectives or adverbs to add greater depth and clarity to the message. This gives the audience a chance to understand more clearly the picture you are depicting, while making it more interesting.

INTENSE LANGUAGE

Language intensity adds strength and power to the message. For example, stating that a concert was inspiring captures the attention of an audience much more readily than saying that it was a "good" concert.

COMPARISONS

Speakers often use comparisons to help the audience better understand their ideas. When you compare an idea in your speech with one that the audience is more familiar with, you have a greater chance of identifying with your audience and of meeting your objective of being clear. Metaphors and similes accomplish this in a more vivid way.

Metaphor

This involves thinking about or experiencing one thing in terms of another by comparing them. For example, life is a journey. Thinking about life as a journey offers a number of opportunities for speakers to make use of concepts associated with a journey such as bumps in the road, growth as a result of new experiences, and so on.

Simile

This is similar to a metaphor except it compares the two items using the words "like" or "as." For example, life is like a journey.

Logic will take you from A to B. Imagination will take you everywhere.

—Albert Einstein

CHAPTER 10

RHYTHMIC DEVICES

Speakers often make use of rhythm in their speeches to create an appealing sound to the listener. This holds their attention longer and, if used properly, can be very compelling to an audience.

Alliteration

This is the repetition of phonetic sounds, usually consonant sounds, at the beginning of words or phrases.

- "In a nation founded on the promise of human dignity, our colleges, our communities, our country should challenge hatred wherever we find it." (Hillary Rodham Clinton)

Antithesis

This is when the speaker pairs two phrases, which sometimes are opposites. More than not, the same words are used for both phrases, but when you change the order of the words in the second phrase it means something different from the first.

- "Ask not what your country can do for you; ask what you can do for your country." (John F. Kennedy)

- "It's not just the strength to get yourself over, but the strength to get over yourself." (U.S. Army)

- "It's not the size of the dog in the fight but the size of the fight in the dog."

Parallelism

This is when you use three or more short, similar series of words, phrases, or sentences that are repeated.

- "I speak as a Republican. I speak as a woman. I speak as a United States Senator. I speak as an American." (Margaret Chase Smith)

- "Free at last, free at last, thank God almighty, we are free at last." (Martin Luther King, Jr.)

Key Terms/Concepts to Know

Language	Quantity
Language rules	Alliteration
Clarity	Antithesis
Relation	Parallelism
Quality	

DELIVERY

CHAPTER OBJECTIVES

This chapter is designed to help you understand:

- How to deliver speeches effectively
- The different methods of delivery
- How to use your voice effectively
- How to use nonverbal communication effectively
- How to design and use visual aids
- How to practice your speech

Photo provided by John William Haas

CHAPTER 11

When you think of any speech, you will think of it as including two components—content and delivery. Delivery is how you present the speech and includes how you sound, how you look, and what you do nonverbally during a presentation. Since delivery is one of the most important parts of the public speaking process, most of us want to know what counts as good or effective speech delivery. As noted by McCroskey (1997), effective delivery includes two basic components: naturalness and conversational quality. These factors are characteristic of effective delivery even though the speech has been rehearsed.

Receivers can be easily distracted by a speaker's voice or body movement. Therefore, a natural speaking style that does not call attention to itself is more effective. It conveys the speaker's ideas in a clear, interesting fashion without distracting the audience. If you speak in a whisper, keep your hands in your pockets, shift your weight side to side, or talk in a monotone voice you will not achieve your goals. Thus, effective speech delivery brings together many separate elements. In this chapter we will explore the factors that contribute to effective delivery. Specifically, we will examine different methods of delivery, the ways speakers can make effective use of their voice, and the ways speakers can make effective use of nonverbal communication.

Methods of Delivery

IMPROMPTU

The first method of delivery is impromptu. You will be delivering two short speeches using this method. An impromptu method of delivery involves little or no preparation. The assignments that require the use of an impromptu method will help you think more quickly and effectively "on your feet." This is not, however, the method that you will use to deliver major speeches such as the informative speech or the persuasive speech. This method is only appropriate when you are put "on the spot" and not when you are expected to be prepared.

READING FROM A MANUSCRIPT

The second method of delivery occurs when a speech is read word-for-word to the audience. Reading from a manuscript is acceptable in special circumstances such as a speech that is delivered by a diplomat to the United Nations General Assembly. In this special kind of setting, it is essential that every word be stated exactly as prepared. This method of delivery is **not** acceptable for use in this class. When you read from a manuscript, you are unable to adapt your message to the audience because reading prevents the speaker from making eye contact with the audience. Effective public speaking requires that the speaker be able to adapt to what the audience is communicating nonverbally.

RECITING FROM MEMORY

The third method of delivery involves reciting your speech from memory, word-for-word. As with reading, reciting from memory is **not** an effective method of delivery. Since the speech is memorized, the speaker is unable to adapt to audience feedback. Moreover, this method is not natural, and tends to distract the audience. It means that every time you practice your speech you use the same words. It makes your voice sound robotic and you will lack vocal variety.

EXTEMPORANEOUS

One of the major goals of this class is to develop your skills as an extemporaneous speaker. An extemporaneous speech is carefully prepared and rehearsed, and is presented from a brief set of notes. Even though it is thoroughly prepared ahead of time, the exact words that the speaker will deliver are not chosen until the moment of delivery. Thus, this style of delivery is quite different than a speech recited from memory. Initially, this style of delivery will seem difficult because you may be tempted to memorize the speech. The key is to not memorize words or even phrases, but to learn or "grasp" the ideas in your speech. As you practice, the same ideas will be discussed, but different words and phrases may be used to describe the same ideas. An effective way of grasping the ideas in your speech is to develop an effective speaking outline and practice!

Perhaps the greatest benefit that a speaker derives from an extemporaneous style of delivery is that it allows the speaker to make use of a natural, **conversational** speaking style. Many people approach public speaking with the idea that it requires a totally different way of communicating. Effective speakers realize that the communication practices that lead to success in interpersonal or group situations apply to public speaking situations. You will speak and use nonverbal communication in much the same way as you would in an ordinary conversation. Approaching your speech with a bit less emphasis on how this setting is different from other communication settings will help you develop an extemporaneous, conversational style of delivery.

Use of Voice

Your voice is very important to your credibility. For the audience to receive your message clearly and without distraction, your voice must be used in a clear, non-distracting manner. There are eight factors involving the use of voice that will influence your performance as well as your grade in this course.

VOLUME

Make sure that you speak loudly enough for all in the room to hear. Many speakers need to project their voice more fully than anticipated in order to be heard by all audience members. This problem can occur because most people are accustomed to speaking in one-on-one or small group settings in which the other party or parties are relatively close to the speaker. In many rooms, sound escapes or is absorbed by the walls, desks, and people. In addition, there may be noise coming from outside the room that overrides your voice. Practice the speech with a more pronounced volume than you expect to use during the presentation. You cannot command audience attention by speaking softly.

RATE

Rate involves the speed with which you speak. The speaker should deliver the speech at a rate or speed that best lends itself to achieving the goal(s) of the presentation. Most students need to slow their speaking rate as a result of nervousness. When we get nervous, we tend to speak faster than we do in natural conversation. When you speak too fast, you do not give your audience time to take in your ideas and understand them. A faster than normal speech rate also impacts negatively on articulation. Speaking at a fast rate causes all the vowel sounds to run together. As a result, you will be very difficult to understand. On the other hand, if you are one of the few who speak too slowly, speak a bit faster so you do not bore your audience. Your objective should be to speak at a rate that maintains audience interest and that does not distract the audience from your message. Seek to be consistent.

ARTICULATION

The physical production of sound is articulation. If you tend to mumble, seek to open your mouth to form words and emphasize the crisp consonant sounds at the beginning and end of words. You do

Photo provided by John William Haas

CHAPTER 11

not want to mush all of your words (vowel sounds) together. Can you think of someone who is difficult to understand because they do not articulate? If you force yourself to articulate, it will also aid you in slowing down your rate of speaking.

PITCH

Another characteristic of the human voice is that it has pitch. Pitch is driven by muscle movements in the speaker's throat. The pitch of a speaker's voice is actually determined by rate of vibration of the vocal cords. As the rate of the vibrations varies, the sound of the voice changes. Faster rates form higher voices, or higher pitches, while slower rates elicit deeper voices, or lower pitches. Thus, pitch involves the highness or lowness of voice.

A "good" pitch is one that is pleasant to the ear and does not distract the audience. Have you ever listened to someone's voice that was so high-pitched that it sounded like fingernails down a chalkboard? Similarly, have you listened to a voice so low that it distracts from the message? If the tone of your voice is too high or low, practice speaking in even tones so that your pitch does not distract your audience.

VOCAL VARIETY

Changes in rate, pitch, and volume that give the voice expressiveness are considered vocal variety. Think about this as the opposite of being monotone. If you read a story to a group of children, you would likely use a lot of inflection in your voice to make it interesting to them. You need to do the same with your speeches to keep your audience interested.

PAUSES

Momentary breaks in vocal delivery are pauses. Short, silent pauses between ideas and/or some sentences are very effective. For example, we understand that a speaker must pause before the punch line of a joke. The pause alerts the listeners to the punch line. Without a pause, the impact of the message is diminished. Pauses not only act as a signal to the audience but they help the speaker manage his/her rate of delivery. Simply put, it forces the speaker to slow down. However, not all pauses are effective.

Vocalized pauses are filler words that you do not want to use in your speech such as "uh," "um," "like," or "you know." Sometimes speakers will also smack their lips, click their tongue, or consistently clear their throat as a vocalized pause. Many of these are nervous habits that the speaker may not be aware of. The more vocalized pauses are used, the less credibility the audience will assign the speaker because they may believe that these are indicators of uncertainty or lack of preparation. Record yourself in order to become aware of how often you use vocalized pauses. Listen to yourself as you speak. As you do this, you will begin to catch yourself before you make use of a vocalized pause. Start replacing these vocalized pauses with silent pauses.

PRONUNCIATION

The culturally accepted standard for the way a word or phrase should be spoken is pronunciation. Make sure you know how to pronounce any and all unfamiliar words, especially the proper names that you cite. If you anticipate difficulty pronouncing a word, find synonyms for it before you begin to practice. Your credibility as a speaker is diminished when you mispronounce words.

DIALECT

The variations of both accent and vocabulary are considered dialect. As a speaker, you will encounter situations in which audience members are not from your hometown, your state, or your country. Individuals in your audience may embrace different cultures and speak with different accents. This course is not designed to change your accent. However, if you know that you possess a strong accent, focus on the other vocal devices discussed above to help your audience understand you. Also, make sure to use grammar correctly and choose your vocabulary carefully. Do not use terms with which your audience may not be familiar. Have others listen to you and offer suggestions on more appropriate forms of grammar and vocabulary where appropriate.

In many cases, one voice-related problem tends to impact on other aspects of a speaker's voice. As you continue through the semester, you will begin to understand which aspects of your voice are considered strengths as well as the aspects of your voice that you need to improve upon.

Nonverbal Communication

Your delivery is not only impacted by your voice but also by your nonverbal cues. Audience members will watch you as well as listen to you. Studies have shown that a speaker's nonverbal communication tends to be viewed as a more accurate indicator of what the speaker is thinking and feeling than the verbal portion of the message. Simply put, we tend to believe what we see rather than what we hear. Consistent with your use of voice, make sure that your nonverbal communication does not distract your audience from the point of the message. For the purposes of this course, we will focus our attention on five nonverbal behaviors that accompany public speaking. You will be graded on your performance in the following areas:

EYE CONTACT

During a speech you will be expected to maintain eye contact with the audience as you speak. Next to an extemporaneous and conversational speaking style, eye contact is the most important factor in the delivery of your speech. Adequate preparation for a speech allows you to use the majority of the time looking at your audience rather than your notes. This is why eye contact is essential to the use of an extemporaneous, conversational speaking style. For example, if you are reading your speech you obviously cannot maintain eye contact with the audience or be able to adapt to the feedback the audience is

Photo provided by John William Haas

CHAPTER 11

providing you. Moreover, DO NOT follow inappropriate prescriptions for dealing with speech anxiety (e.g., don't look at the audience, find a point at the back of the room and focus on it). Instead, maintain approximately equal eye contact with all members of the audience. Practice scanning the room back and forth. Your eyes should convey confidence, sincerity and conviction. Effective speakers maintain eye contact with the audience throughout the presentation. Whatever the length of the presentation, eye contact with the audience should be maintained for approximately 70–80 percent of the speech.

HAND GESTURES

Gestures involve the motions of both your hands and arms. Effective gestures are natural and do not call attention to themselves. Ineffective gestures are robotic, overdone, and unnatural. Ineffective gesturing includes clenching the podium, putting your hands in your pockets, waving your hands excessively, or clasping your hands behind your back. Many students find that they do not know what to do with their hands while speaking. If you naturally use many hand gestures, try placing your notes on the podium so that you can effectively gesture.

BODILY ACTION

While gestures include both hands and arms, bodily action is everything else that your body does. We usually associate bodily action with posture and weight distribution. Speakers vary in how they use their body during the course of a speech. For some, their body movement distracts the audience. The kind of distracting mannerisms speakers should avoid include swaying back and forth, tapping a foot, and pacing. To keep from distracting your audience, practice good posture by standing with your feet a little more than shoulder-width apart while maintaining equal weight on each foot. This posture will keep you from swaying or bouncing, since the weight on both legs is evenly distributed. If you practice this at home, it will become more natural to you when you deliver your speeches in class, thus giving you more confidence and credibility.

FACIAL EXPRESSION

Your facial expressions can tell the audience about your mood, thoughts, and feelings. You want the message that you convey through your face to be the same as the verbal message you send. For example, if you are conveying enthusiasm about a new product, you want that emotion to be communicated through your face. Many times, when students should convey excitement about the message, they appear to be miserable when delivering their speech. Since your nonverbal behaviors are more believable than your verbal behaviors, both should match.

PERSONAL APPEARANCE

You will not be viewed as a credible speaker unless you look the part. If you look professional you will perform in a more professional manner. For the purposes of this course, you are expected to wear business casual attire. Business casual attire DOES NOT include the kind of clothes that you might wear on a social occasion such as when you go to a club or to a party. Rather, business casual attire for males includes slacks, a shirt with a collar, socks, and non-athletic shoes. For women, it is an outfit that includes sleeves and slacks or a dress/ skirt that has a modest hemline. Do not wear:

- Athletic apparel
- Jeans
- Clothing with holes
- Sandals/flip flops
- Shorts

In addition, there are several other items about your appearance to consider. For males, tuck shirts into pants and do not role up shirt sleeves. For women, limit the accessories that you wear (earrings, bracelets, etc.) to items that will not draw attention away from your message.

Remember that others are judging your credibility based, in part, on nonverbal cues from the time you leave your seat until the time you return. Therefore, your nonverbal behavior should be composed both before and after your speech. Since delivery is such a large component of your speech grade, you should practice with the goal of combining all of the factors we have discussed in this chapter. Practice does not always make perfect, but it does make permanent.

Using Visual Aids

Visual aids are an important but controversial component of public speaking. The decision to use visual aids should be driven by whether or not the visual aids help the speaker achieve his/her goals. Thus, if you choose to use visual aids for a speech in this course, you must make sure that they are necessary and that you are not just using them as a substitute for speech content.

In this course, you will be taught how to use visual aids only to enhance your speech. That is, they advance your speaking goals and objectives by adding to your speech. They should never dictate any content in your speech or replace any portions of your speech. The speech itself should stand alone, verbally. Many students make this mistake when choosing, preparing, and presenting visual aids. When you use a visual aid, you will be evaluated in the following ways. First, did you choose the appropriate visual aid(s) for the kind of information you are seeking to visually represent? Second, how well prepared is the visual? Third, how well did you present the visual aid(s) during your speech? Please note: If you do not use a visual aid, you will be graded on whether one was needed for your speech.

WHEN TO USE VISUAL AIDS

There are three major reasons for using visual aids. However, visual aids are not necessary or even appropriate for all speeches. When deciding when to use a visual aid, ask yourself if its use will advance your objectives in the following ways:

CHAPTER 11

Adding Clarity

Since one of the major goals of any type of speech is to be clear, this is the primary advantage of using visual aids. There may be portions of your speech that are difficult to explain or describe. Visual aids are effective tools for clarifying complex ideas that do not lend themselves to simple, clear language. If your visual aids are not clear, they will not only be useless but they will actually detract from your speech.

Adding Interest

Visual aids are often used to attract attention to a piece of information as well as spark curiosity about sub-topics. Look over your outline and consider whether some areas of your speech are not as interesting as others. In such cases, you may want to add a visual aid to strengthen the supporting material used in that portion of the speech.

Aiding in Retention

You may also want to pick out material in your speech that you want to stand out and make memorable. Visual aids that make use of images tend to be more memorable than visuals that rely on words or phrases. Using a visual aid in this instance will give you a better chance of meeting your goals.

TYPES OF VISUAL AIDS

There are several types of visual aids that are used in public speaking. Visual aids should not be chosen based on what is easy to prepare or what you have directly at your disposal. Instead, **your selection and use of visual aids will be determined by the information/supporting material in the body of your speech**. You may use a combination of the following types of visual aids:

Objects

One way to clarify ideas and provide a dramatic impact is to bring an object of what you are discussing. For example, if you are talking about biking you may want to use biking equipment as visual aids. Keep in mind when you bring in objects that they should be large enough for the audience to see yet small enough to be suitable for the speech setting. Also, remember that objects such as live animals, firearms, or illegal substances are not permitted and are against university policy.

Models

A model is either a small-scale replica of a large object, a large-scale replica of a small object, or life-size representation of the real object. For example, if you were giving a speech about the portions of a building, you may want to bring a model of it. If the object is too small for the audience to see you may want to find or make a model of it. For example, a speech about how to administer CPR may require a dummy for demonstration purposes.

Photographs

Photos often aid a speaker when there is a need to present an image of an individual, place, or event. Photographs must be presented using presentation software such as PowerPoint® in order for your audience to view it properly.

Diagrams/Drawings

Sketches, diagrams, and illustrations are all types of drawings that, when prepared properly, can be a very effective way to demonstrate your point precisely. These are used when there is not a photograph of the item, or a photograph does not show the item well enough. For example, if you need to show the human heart or lungs, a diagram would label the various parts. A speech about plans for a future building may include an architectural drawing of floor plans. If explaining dyslexia to an audience, the speaker may prepare a drawing of what a sentence looks like to those with dyslexia. In addition, a drawing would help in a situation where you were discussing theories of how JFK was assassinated. The video or photographs do not show the trajectory of the bullets but when drawn out, the audience would better understand the angle. Like photographs, diagrams should be displayed using presentation software such as PowerPoint®.

Graphs

Graphs are useful ways of clarifying quantitative data and making visible relationships between numbers. The three types of graphs are used to clarify quantitative data: line graphs, bar graphs, and pie graphs. Whenever a speaker uses multiple numbers as supporting information, it would be appropriate to place these numbers in a form that the audience can follow, such as graphs. The type of graph you choose to use as a visual aid will depend on the type of quantitative data that is being used.

- **Line graph**—uses two or more lines to show trends or statistics over time or space. For example, a line graph would be used to show the federal government revenues and outlays from 1981 to 2010.

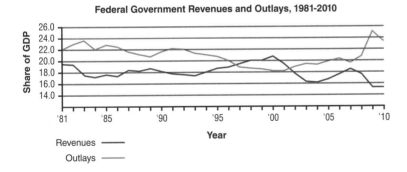

CHAPTER 11

- **Bar graph**—uses vertical or horizontal bars to compare two or more numerical items. For example, a bar graph would be used to compare spending on scientific research and development.

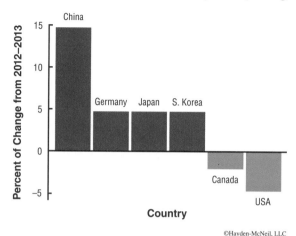

Scientific Research and Development Spending

©Hayden-McNeil, LLC

- **Pie graph**—emphasizes portions of a circle to show distribution patterns of numbers, that is, portions of a whole. For example, you would use a pie graph to show the areas of spending for the federal government.

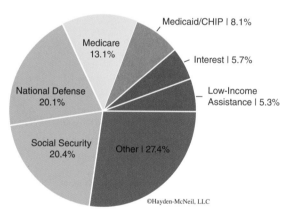

2010 Federal Spending

©Hayden-McNeil, LLC

As with photographs and diagrams, graphs should be displayed using presentation software.

Video/Audio Clips

You should choose to show a clip from a movie, commercial, documentary, television show, or YouTube if you want to show a demonstration of someone's behavior or how something works. This is, of course, if you cannot demonstrate it yourself. Choosing to use a videotape may complicate the preparation process for many reasons. First, the timing associated with the use of the visual needs to be calculated to make sure you have enough time in your speech for the clip. Second, other visual aids allow you to talk while you are displaying them, but unless you mute the video you do not have that luxury. Third, make use of short clips from a videotape. You are taking away from the time available to you as a speaker when using this type of visual aid. Fourth, make sure to have the video cued up to the scene you wish to show. Fifth, work with the equipment in advance so you can easily play and stop the video during your speech so as not to interrupt the flow of your speech or distract the audience. Last, set the desired volume before speeches begin. Because you cannot talk about the clip while it is being played, unless it is muted, you will have to explain before the clip what your audience is about to see and explain what we viewed after the clip is played.

Handouts

Finally, depending on your information, there may be something that you will need to give your audience to keep and take home with them. In this case, you will want to construct and bring a handout to give them at the end of your speech. For example, if you were persuading your audience to become organ donors, it would be necessary to give them organ donor cards. If you are persuading your audience not to drink and drive and are talking about alternatives such as calling a taxi, you would need to give your audience a small sheet with taxi phone numbers for them to keep in their wallet/purse. If you must use a handout, allow the audience time to read it before proceeding. Seek to manage how the audience will use the handout while it is in their possession.

PREPARING VISUAL AIDS

While the first portion of the visual aid grade focuses on your choice of visual aid, the second portion concerns how effectively you prepare your visual aid. Follow the guidelines below for preparing your visual aids.

Preparing All Types of Visual Aids

- **Prepare visual aids after preparing your speech.** DO NOT prepare visual aids or even decide upon them until your ENTIRE speech is complete. When your speech is complete go through your preparation outline and decide where a visual is needed and what type to prepare. If you consider or prepare visual aids before your speech is complete, it will begin to dictate your speech and become your speech. Remember, visual aids are only used to enhance your speech.

- **Prepare visual aids before you practice.** If you wait until the last day before your speech to "throw in" a visual aid, you will not have time to practice with it, which can throw off timing and flow, and inevitably take away from your credibility.

- **Keep visual aids simple.** You are not in a contest to see who can have the most elaborate visual aid. Less is more! If your goal is to be clear to your audience then keep it simple. Elaborate visual aids are distracting and confusing to your audience. If it takes your audience more than a few seconds to determine what your visual aid represents, it is not simple enough.

CHAPTER 11

- **Make sure visual aids are large enough.** Your visual aid will not clarify information, increase interest, or help your listeners retain your message if audience members cannot see it. It will also decrease your credibility. Bring your visual aid into class before the day of your speech to try it out from the back of the room to test its size and ability to be seen. For this reason, you should add pictures, graphs, and so on to PowerPoint® slides. This will ensure that it will be large enough for everyone in your audience to see.

Preparing PowerPoint® Slides

- **Never use full sentences.** The most important guideline to preparing PowerPoint® slides and the biggest mistake that students make is to use too much text on slides. Do not force your audience to read your speech! It is your responsibility as a speaker to give them the information verbally. The only place that text is needed for PowerPoint® slides is for titles, citations or charts. Remember that the main reason we use visual aids in the first place is to help clarify information—not to cause more work for our listeners.

- **Use color effectively.** Use a limited number of colors on slides. Too many colors may create a distraction. Use one color for titles and another color for text. If you choose a dark background, use light-colored text. When creating a graph, make sure that every portion is a separate color and that these colors do not clash with the background.

- **Choose font types wisely.** Avoid using decorative and distracting fonts that are difficult to read. Times New Roman and Courier tend to be more readily followed by the audience. Choose one kind of font and use it consistently throughout all slides. You also should avoid placing the text in all capital letters.

- **Make font sizes large enough.** You must use a font size that is large enough to be seen by your entire audience. Usually the font that is given on a new slide is appropriate. A large enough font to be seen clearly is 44 point for titles and 32 point for text. For citations, you may want to use a 28-point font. However, any font smaller than this and your audience will be straining to see.

- **Be consistent with all slides.** The background, font, and colors that you choose for slides should be consistent throughout the presentation. Consistency makes it easier for the audience to read and recognize the information on the slides faster. Remember, keep it simple.

- **Use space effectively.** Avoid large blank spaces on a slide. Try to use the entire slide or combine information onto one slide. In addition, do not put too much material on a single slide. You do not want to force your audience to look at multiple items at once. Also, leave extra room at the edge of slides so the information will not be cut off by the equipment.

- **Avoid sound.** Make sure that the sound is off under the animation function or on the equipment you use. Any unnecessary sound will only distract you and your audience. Again, keep it simple.

- **Avoid unnecessary animation.** In PowerPoint®, custom animation allows you to have your text and graphics appear through decorative animation such as scrolling or flying into the slide. You need to make sure when you custom animate your slides under slide show, you click on "appear" for timing so the information only appears when you advance your slides. Any other animation will distract your audience.

- **Avoid timing your slides.** Never time your slides so they scroll through without your cue. This will dictate your speech and make it difficult to adapt to feedback or change course during your speech when necessary. You want the setting to be manual so you can click to the next slide when you are ready.

- **Avoid clip art.** There is no reason that you will need to use clip art—it is unnecessary. You should be able to find on the Web actual photos or images of anything you need to illustrate your point.

- **Avoid a title slide.** You are asked to begin your speech by gaining the audience's attention, not with your topic, so it is inappropriate to include the title of the speech and your name on the first slide. You should begin the first slide with either a blank slide or whatever you are choosing as your attention-gaining device, if necessary.

- **Use blank slides when necessary.** A blank slide is needed anywhere that you are not discussing a visual aid. You should also add a blank slide at the beginning and end of the presentation to meet this guideline.

- **Write presentation cues on speaking outline.** To remind yourself when to change slides, you should include cues on your speaking outline. If you have several slides you may want to print out the slides and write your speaking outline within the pages.

A visual aid tutorial and PowerPoint® tutorial is available on the school website listed on your syllabus. The tutorial will show you what PowerPoint® slides should and should not look like.

CHAPTER 11

PRESENTING VISUAL AIDS

In addition to selection and preparation, the use of visual aids will have considerable impact on the outcome of the speech and your visual aid grade. Your use of visual aids must conform to the following guidelines (Lucas, 2001):

- **Avoid using the chalkboard/whiteboard.** Using the chalkboard or whiteboard is not appropriate in a formal speech for four major reasons. First, it forces you to turn your back to the audience and lose eye contact and volume. Second, it takes valuable time from your speech. Third, it is messy. Last, it shows the audience that you have not taken the time and effort to prepare your visual aid in advance, which lessens your credibility and appears unprofessional.

- **Display them where listeners can see them.** Make sure that whatever visual aid you use, everyone in your audience can view it. If you are showing your audience an object or model you must place your object up high enough for all to see without moving it around and leave it up long enough for people to view it properly. Do not hold the object in front of your face but over your head. If you are demonstrating something make sure you stand out from behind the podium in the center of the room, giving everyone a better chance of seeing what you are demonstrating.

- **Avoid passing them among the audience.** If you have a handout you want your audience to keep, you must wait until the end of your speech to hand it out. The best time to do this is after your final statement and before you ask for questions. You do not want to pass anything among your audience before or during your speech because it will take the attention away from you and your speech while also distracting you and your audience. If you have pictures, graphs, and so on that you just want the audience to see, place them in PowerPoint® slides during your speech.

- **Display only while discussing them.** It is very important that you only show visual aids while you are discussing them. After you have moved on from the idea and visual aid to illustrate it, take it down or advance the slide to either the next piece of information or a blank slide. In addition, do not show the visual aid until you are ready to discuss it in your speech.

- **Explain each clearly and concisely.** You cannot display a visual aid and discuss a topic that is different from what is visible. You must explain to your audience what the visual represents. Do not assume that your audience knows what the graph or photograph represents.

- **Talk to your audience, not the visual aid.** You should maintain eye contact with your audience even when showing and explaining a visual aid. If you are using PowerPoint®, we encourage you to print out your slides and write your speaking outline within it so you are looking at the same thing that your audience sees. You should practice the speech with your visual aids enough times so that you know, when you advance a slide, what will appear on the screen.

- **Practice with your visual aids.** The only way to ensure you are following the preceding guidelines is to incorporate visual aids into your speech while you are practicing, so that it flows and is not distracting. You must be able to make a smooth transition between visual aids without unnatural pauses. If you do not practice with the visuals while rehearsing your speech, their use will take more time than expected and it will reduce your credibility.

Rehearsing Your Speech

After you have completed the entire speech-making process you must give yourself ample time to practice the speech. Do not wait until the night before the speech to begin rehearsing. You should have your preparation outline converted to a speaking outline (your notes) and have visual aids already incorporated before you begin practicing. The more you rehearse the more prepared you will feel. This feeling of being prepared will help to reduce nervousness and will further your credibility. The following steps, when followed, will enhance your practice time.

- Read the speaking outline aloud several times, adding any material you need.

- Talk through all examples and stories, especially the ones you are very familiar with (think of how you want to tell them), so you do not ramble through them.

- Recite in full all quotations, and work out the wording of statistics.

- Use visual aids as you practice so you become comfortable presenting them.

- Now, you are ready to practice the entire speech from start to finish. If you run into problems, push yourself to keep going and practice the entire speech so your speech will be equally polished from introduction to conclusion. If not, the introduction will seem better developed than the rest of your speech.

- As you practice, concentrate on gaining control of the ideas instead of trying to learn the speech word for word. If you follow this practice, your speaking style will be more extemporaneous and conversational.

- Next, begin to time yourself every time you practice the speech from beginning to end. Each time you rehearse, your speech time should be approximately the same. If you are exceeding your speech time, you will need to go back and **condense** the information based on the following criteria.

  - First, find passages where you are repeating yourself

  - Second, **eliminate clutter** which includes any information that is not directly related to achieving your goals

  - Third, assign a priority to each information item in the speech and begin to eliminate the items with the lowest priority

CHAPTER 11

- At this point, begin to polish and refine your delivery by practicing both vocal and nonverbal components by standing behind something that resembles a podium. Rehearse by standing the way you would in the classroom and holding up your notes. Use the same volume, vocal variety, and rate that would be appropriate in the classroom. If you have visual aids, place them in the same location around you as they will be in the classroom. The more realistic your practice setting, the better you will perform.

- Record the speech to gauge volume, vocal variety, rate, pauses, and clear language use.

- Practice your speech in front of friends, roommates, and family. Seek honest feedback about the speech and consider making changes based on this input.

Addressing Audience Questions

There may be a brief question-and-answer session immediately following your informative and persuasive speeches. It will be your responsibility as a speaker, after you finish the final statement of your speech, to ask the audience if there are any questions. Throughout the preparation of your speech you can begin to formulate answers to possible questions from the audience. When preparing for the question-and-answer session, consider the following guidelines.

- Take this part of the event as seriously as the speech itself. Your speech begins from the time you leave your seat and does not end until you return to it.

- Use the same conversational delivery style that you used for the speech itself. Do not become someone different after your speech has concluded.

- Approach questions with a positive attitude. Do not assume that your classmates' aim is to embarrass you or trip you up. Most of the questions asked simply originate from peers' curiosity. As a group you have created an environment of support. Remember, do unto others as you would have done to you.

- Listen carefully to the question that is being asked. It is tempting for your mind to race through all of the things you think you may have done or left out of your speech, and that may lead to not paying attention to the question.

- Answer the question that has been asked. A credible speaker focuses directly on the question asked and addresses it to the best of his or her ability.

- Repeat the question for the entire audience before you answer if you believe that the question was not heard by everyone. This will help every listener to feel as involved as they did during the speech.

- Direct your answers to the entire audience and not just the person who asked the question. This practice will help you to involve the entire audience and make them feel like active participants. If you only answer the one person, the communication changes from a public context to an interpersonal one. This will create an uncomfortable atmosphere where there will be several conversations taking place at once and attention taken away from you, the speaker.

- Be honest and straightforward. If you do not know the answer to a question, do not pretend that you do by making up something. Your audience is certain to discover your dishonesty and lose their trust in you as a credible speaker. If you do not know an answer, simply respond by indicating that it was not part of your research.

Key Terms/Concepts to Know

Impromptu delivery	Eye contact
Reading from a manuscript	Hand gestures
Memorized	Facial expression
Extemporaneous	Personal appearance
Naturalness	Using visual aids
Conversational quality	Constructing visual aids
Use of voice	Practice

Reference List

McCroskey, J.C. (1997). *An introduction to rhetorical communication* (7th ed.). Boston: Allyn & Bacon.

CHAPTER 11

UNIT 3

TYPES OF SPEECHES

INFORMATIVE SPEAKING

CHAPTER OBJECTIVES

This chapter is designed to help you understand:

- The different types of informative speeches

- Informative speeches about objects, processes, events, and concepts

- How to deliver an effective informative speech

Photo provided by John William Haas

The general purpose for your first major scholarly speech is to inform. For an informative speech you will be sharing your knowledge of the topic but you are not there to "teach." Rather, your goal is to assist the audience in becoming as familiar and knowledgeable of the topic as you have become. After writing a specific purpose statement, you should then determine the type of informative speech you plan to deliver.

Types of Informative Speeches

Once your purpose is established, you will need to decide what type of informative speech you will be presenting. This decision will determine other aspects of the preparation process, such as organization. For the purposes of this course, your informative speech will be about an international topic. This speech on an international topic may involve an object, process, event, or concept.

OBJECTS

Informative speeches about objects include anything visible and tangible. Speeches about objects can include people, places, and things. Keep in mind that this object must have an international focus.

- Specific Purpose: To inform my audience about the three major accomplishments in the life of Margaret Thatcher as the British Prime Minister.

- Specific Purpose: To inform my audience about the five major sections of the Taj Mahal.

PROCESSES

Informative speeches about processes include any series of steps or stages that lead to a specific result or product. These are usually how-to speeches. Keep in mind that this process must have an international focus.

- Specific Purpose: To inform my audience about the property buying process in South Africa.

- Specific Purpose: To inform my audience about the process of applying for admission to Beijing University in China.

EVENTS

Informative speeches about events include occasions, incidents, or episodes. Usually an event has a beginning and an end, even if the end has not yet occurred. Keep in mind that this event must have an international focus.

- Specific Purpose: To inform my audience about the fall of the Berlin Wall.

- Specific Purpose: To inform my audience about the 2014 FIFA World Cup.

CONCEPTS

Informative speeches about concepts include any belief, theory, idea, notion, or principle. By process of elimination, if the purpose is not an object, process, or event, it will be a concept. Keep in mind that this concept must have an international focus.

- Specific Purpose: To inform my audience about German conceptions of good customer service.

Criteria for Effective Informative Speaking
COMMUNICATE INFORMATION CLEARLY

Sharing information clearly is your top priority when delivering an informative speech. Your goal should not be to appear smarter than your audience. To accomplish this, use simple terms and concepts to explain your ideas. You do not want them to be more confused at the end of your speech than they were before your speech. If you already know a great deal about your topic you may find it difficult to "dumb down" more technical information in terms they identify with. It is a mistake to envision the speech process as the same as the process that you use to write a paper. For example, when you read a paper and do not understand something, you can go back and read it again or refer to an earlier portion of the paper. In a speech, your audience does not have that luxury. They experience the speech only once. They cannot rewind you and they do not have your outline in front of them. Therefore, preparing a speech is much different from writing a paper for the following reasons regarding clarity:

- Spoken language should be more redundant. In a paper, it is often appropriate to find different ways to say something, and to use synonyms for words that are used repeatedly. In a speech, however, you should use the same terms for your topic, main points, and so on so the audience can identify with them. Research suggests that we need to hear something several times before we begin to identify with it and remember it. You do not want to confuse your audience with different terms.

- Spoken language should be less complex. In a paper, many students try to use long, technical terms to give it an intelligent voice. In a speech, you must use the shortest, clearest terms when attempting to explain a concept. If your audience has to stop and dwell on the meaning of an unfamiliar term, they are bound to miss some information along the way.

- Explanations in speeches should be reduced. In papers, we sometimes attempt to draw out information and explain the same concept in many ways, extending the length of the paper. In a speech, the opposite should be true. Why would you take four to five sentences to explain what you can get across in one sentence? As a speaker, you want to get to the point quickly, be clear, and move on.

COMMUNICATE INFORMATION ACCURATELY

Make sure that you are conveying the supporting materials truthfully and accurately to your listeners. You will be expected to check all information before you report them in your speech.

MAKE INFORMATION RELEVANT TO THE AUDIENCE

You will be expected to explain to the audience why the material you are presenting should mean something to them and why they should learn the information. Make clear to the audience how the topic affects them and how they can use it.

Photo provided by John William Haas

CHAPTER 12

Photo provided by John William Haas

Guidelines for Effective Informative Speaking

As you prepare your informative speech, the following guidelines should be followed in order to be effective in reaching your overall goal.

DO NOT OVERESTIMATE WHAT THE AUDIENCE KNOWS

It is easy to assume that because you know a lot about the topic that your audience does, too. However, in many cases this is not a valid assumption. You will become an "expert" with the content of your speech but you must take a step back in order to begin to understand how to share basic information with your audience. Remember that they are hearing much of this information for the first time and they only hear it once.

RELATE THE SUBJECT DIRECTLY TO THE AUDIENCE

Your speech must not be generic in nature. You will tailor the content of the speech to your specific audience. If that audience were to change, you would need to adapt your message to new demographic and situational factors.

DO NOT BE TOO TECHNICAL

Avoid using technical terms that your audience will not understand. As you are searching for information, consider paraphrasing complicated information in order for your audience to comprehend the content faster and easier. Many students like to use very technical terms when writing papers and feel that they must do the same in a speech. However, if clarity is the goal, then you want to use the simplest terms possible so the audience will not be confused.

AVOID ABSTRACTIONS

The first goal of informative speaking is to be clear. Therefore, make sure you explain your information thoroughly. The best way to avoid being abstract is to use description by comparing and contrasting your ideas. Compare or contrast the concept with something the audience is already familiar with. Using examples will help to do this. You could say "it is like this" or "it is different in this way."

PERSONALIZE YOUR IDEAS

Present your thoughts in human terms that relate to the experiences of the audience. Do not be afraid to use your own experiences to bring life to your information. You want the audience to identify with you and your speech, so learn what experiences are common to you and the audience members.

Organizing the Informative Speech

Previously, we discussed the process of organizing a speech in general terms. In this chapter, we are concerned with choosing a specific organizational pattern for the informative speech. Speeches that deal with process have a fairly obvious organizational structure (chronological) but other types of speeches may have additional organizing options.

The organizing pattern should be selected based on what best supports the speech objective. Along with the speech objective, you should also ask yourself what the audience will find most difficult to follow. Considering the question will aid you in choosing an organizational pattern because you will be able to arrange the speech in such a way as to overcome potential problems with comprehension. The most common organizing patterns that are used in informative speeches include chronological, topical, and spatial. In addition, informative topics occasionally lend themselves to a cause and effect pattern of organizing.

Photo provided by John William Haas

INFORMATIVE SPEECH ORGANIZING PATTERN CHECKLIST

- Use a chronological pattern if the information that you are presenting is historical or involves a series of steps that occur in sequence.

- Use a spatial pattern if the information that you are presenting involves physical space or how objects may be physically related (e.g., the layout of a building).

- Use a topical pattern if the information that you are presenting is divided into classes or subgroups.

- Use a cause and effect pattern if the information you are presenting involves why something happens and what is the result when this thing happens.

Key Terms/Concepts to Know

Types of informative speeches

Speeches about objects

Speeches about processes

Speeches about events

Speeches about concepts

Guidelines for effective informative speaking

CHAPTER 12

STUDENT NOTES

PERSUASIVE SPEAKING

CHAPTER OBJECTIVES

This chapter is designed to help you understand:

- How to define persuasion

- How persuasion works

- The different types of persuasive speeches

- The organizational patterns associated with persuasive speeches

- How to build persuasive arguments

People experience many persuasive messages on a daily basis. You are the target of persuasive messages and you target others with persuasive messages as well. You may try to talk your friend into going out, ask your parents for money, or watch ads on TV trying to persuade you to buy a product or purchase a service. In some instances, the goal(s) of the sender are achieved.

In most cases, the audience rejects the persuasive appeal. For people in a wide variety of careers including government and politics, public relations, advertising, sales, management, and coaching, persuasive speaking skills are a necessary ingredient for success. Thus, it is not surprising that many people are interested in knowing more about persuasion and how it works. In this chapter we will define persuasion, discuss how persuasion is believed to work, and describe how to develop persuasive arguments.

CHAPTER 13

Persuasion Defined

Like communication, persuasion has been a difficult concept to define. Most agree that persuasion should be defined as involving some measure of change in attitudes and/or behaviors. In addition, most all definitions agree that persuasion is a **receiver-oriented** area of study. That is, our principal concern is with how messages impact the receiver. However, there is less agreement on other aspects of a definition of persuasion. Consider the following questions:

- Is the message considered "persuasion" if the speaker does not achieve his/her objectives? The answer to this question has very practical implications. If you believe that persuasion should be defined so that the speaker must achieve his/her goals in changing attitudes or behaviors, how do you view an unsuccessful attempt at changing the attitudes or behaviors of the audience? Is it success or is it the attempt to persuade that should fall within our definition? What should your grade be on the persuasive speaking assignment if you deliver a good speech but fail to influence the attitudes or behaviors of audience members?

- Is the message considered "persuasion" when the sender does not act in good faith and make clear his/her intentions? If a speaker influences you to change behaviors for "your own good" but the speaker's true intention is to benefit himself/herself, has persuasion taken place?

At its core, **persuasion** involves the changing or reinforcing of attitudes and/or behaviors. We will adopt the working definition used by O'Keefe (1990) for persuasion as the intentional influencing of receivers' attitudes and/or behaviors through communication.

HOW PERSUASION WORKS

Persuasion takes place when messages influence the attitudes and/or behaviors of receivers. However, no one has actually "seen" how persuasion works. That is, no one has actually viewed what a message does when it collides with an attitude that exists in your mind. Researchers have developed a wide range of theories that attempt to explain what happens when persuasion occurs. One way to understand this body of theory and research on persuasion and how it works is to examine the key factors that make a difference when persuasion is taking place. Effective public speakers understand that these factors will impact their ability to achieve persuasive objectives. These factors will be particularly important to consider when you are seeking to influence the **target audience**.

The target audience consists of the group of people that you are most interested in influencing during the speech—that is, the portion of the whole audience you most want to persuade. For example, students often target teachers during in-class presentations since teachers assign grades and classmates do not. However, because audience relevance is so much more important in a persuasive speech, it is imperative that you, as a speaker, determine your target audience. Regardless of skill level, it is difficult for a speaker to persuade all audience members.

Since the act of persuasion deals with people's attitudes or behaviors it is unrealistic to think that your speech will influence every audience member the way in which you desire. Determining your target audience will help you establish a realistic goal for yourself. Consider diagramming your target audience as shown/explained below.

Before the Speech

Opposing
Position(s)

Your
Position

©Hayden-McNeil, LLC

After the Speech

Opposing
Position(s)

Your
Position

Target Audience Attitude Change Model

The solid line represents a range of views on a particular topic. The poles on the solid line represent your position on a topic and opposing positions on a topic. The dots represent audience members and where they stand in their attitudes or behaviors regarding your topic. The ? in the middle represents people who are unsure, do not know, do not care, or do not have an opinion. The members of the audience plotted on the right side of the figure already agree with you or are currently doing what you seek. Thus, you are reinforcing their attitudes or behaviors through your speech. Therefore, your target audience includes all audience members, some of whom disagree with your position and others who do not. As noted, it would be unrealistic to assume that all audience members will move to the right side by the end of your speech. If persuasion deals with change, then your goal should be to bring each person closer to your side. This means that the listeners on the left side of the diagram should be closer to the middle and considering the possibility of changing their attitudes or behaviors.

Types of Persuasive Speeches/ Organizational Patterns

There are several different types of persuasive speeches. For many people, persuasive speeches are put into categories on the basis of the type of question the speaker is seeking to answer. The use of questions underscores the role of controversy in persuasion. There is often more than one answer to a question. The three different types of persuasive speeches are designed to address questions of fact, questions of value, and questions of policy.

CHAPTER 13

Photo provided by John William Haas

QUESTIONS OF FACT

Persuasive speeches that address questions of fact focus on the truth of a claim or assertion. Simply put, the persuasive speech attempts to answer "what is." This may seem to contradict our earlier discussion that facts are beyond dispute. In this type of persuasive presentation, the speaker is asserting that the label (fact) we have assigned to some kind of information is not valid or that previously unlabeled information should be assigned the label "fact." Facts about the physical world are easier to establish than facts about our social world. A **topical** pattern of organization is best suited to persuasive speeches designed to address questions of fact. The main points in the body of your speech should be the reasons why the fact is true or false (your arguments).

- Specific Purpose: To persuade my audience that global warming is underway.

- Central Idea: The four major reasons that global warming is taking place include sea level rise, global temperature rise, warming oceans, and shrinking ice sheets.

QUESTIONS OF VALUE

Persuasive speeches that address questions of value focus on the worth or importance we attach to an idea or action. Moreover, this type of persuasive speech calls upon the audience to make a judgment as to the worth of an idea or action. Usually it seeks to persuade the audience that something is good or bad or right or wrong. However, many times it seeks to compare by persuading the audience that something is better than something else or the best option. A **topical** pattern of organization is best suited to persuasive speeches designed to address questions of value. The main points in the body of your speech should be the reasons why it is good or bad, right or wrong, or better or the best (your arguments).

- Specific Purpose: To persuade my audience that marijuana should be legalized.

- Central Idea: The three major reasons why marijuana should be legalized are that criminalization has not deterred use, marijuana has medicinal value, and its legal use could generate new revenue to support economic and social programs.

QUESTIONS OF POLICY

Persuasive speeches that address questions of policy focus on change. When choosing a question of policy speech, you must decide whether your goal is to gain passive agreement or to stimulate immediate action. There are two major organizational patterns that are appropriate for a question of policy speech. A **problem–solution** pattern of organization uses two main points. The first is the problem(s) or why change is needed, and the second is the solution(s) or what you are proposing. In addition, a sequential speech pattern known as **Monroe's Motivational Sequence** is the recommended pattern to use because it follows a logical pattern of thought and ensures that you include all aspects in your persuasive message. This pattern will be discussed below. In both of these patterns the reasons are not main points but the sub-points under the first main point in the body.

Question of Policy to Gain Passive Agreement:
- Specific Purpose: To persuade my audience that a state law is needed to prohibit the use of cell phones while driving.

- Central Idea (problem–solution): Today I will discuss the reasons why a state law is needed to prohibit the use of cell phones while driving, and how the law will work.

- Specific Purpose: To persuade my audience that Hope Scholarships should be available to all students in good academic standing.

- Central Idea (Monroe's Motivational Sequence): Today I will show you the reasons why Hope Scholarships should be available to all UT students who are in good academic standing, alternatives to current scholarship award practices, and the benefits to changing the program for UT students.

Question of Policy to Gain Immediate Action:
- Specific Purpose: To persuade my audience to boycott coffee that is not Rainforest Alliance Certified.

- Central Idea (problem–solution): Today I will show you the reasons why you should boycott coffee that is not Rainforest Certified, and how you can purchase coffee that is certified.

Monroe's Motivational Sequence

As mentioned before, Monroe's Motivational Sequence is an organizational pattern for persuasive speeches as an alternative for problem–solution. It is popular with many speakers because it offers a clear series of steps to follow when developing and delivering a persuasive message (McKerrow, Gronbeck, & Monroe, 2000). The advantage of using this sequence is that it provides listeners with a clearly structured message that tends to follow the way receivers process messages. As shown above, it should only be used for persuasive speeches on question of policy. Below are the five steps to Monroe's Motivational Sequence, the order of the steps, the purpose of each step, and where each step is found in your speech.

INTRODUCTION
- **Attention** (first main point). You must first gain the **attention** and interest of your listeners in the introduction of your speech just as you did in your informative speech.

BODY
- **Need** (second main point). During the need step you must explain the reasons why change is needed. The speaker must convince the audience that there is a serious problem with the existing situation that requires this change. It is important to relate to values and experiences of the audience during the need phase of the speech. It is in this step of the persuasive speech that you will answer most audience objections.

Don't raise your voice, improve your argument.

—Desmond Tutu

CHAPTER 13

> *To accomplish great things we must first dream, then visualize, then plan... believe... act!*
>
> —Alfred A. Montapert

- **Satisfaction** (third main point). In the satisfaction phase of the speech, you will propose solution(s) to the problem(s) identified in the need phase of the speech. You will present an in-depth plan in this phase to make clear how and why the plan would work. If you are attempting to gain passive agreement, you will explain exactly how this change can and would be made (how it works). If you are attempting to gain immediate action, it will be necessary to explain how to do it, who to contact, where to go, and so on. If asking your audience to refrain from doing something, this section should focus on providing the audience with alternatives to this behavior.

- **Visualization** (fourth main point). Benefits are explained in this step by showing what will be improved if your solution is adopted. You will also use analogical reasoning in this phase of the speech to illustrate how your solution has worked in a similar situation. In many cases, these benefits will seem very similar to the information in the need section. If this is the case, it may be advantageous for you to use problem–solution for your organizational pattern.

CONCLUSION

- **Action** (fifth main point). After you recap your main points, remind the audience of the need for change and what you want them to do prior to delivering the final statement. This ensures that the audience will not lose sight of the purpose.

On the next page is an excerpt of an outline showing what you should include in a persuasive speech that is question of policy. This will help you determine what research to find and act as a formula in which you can place your information.

I. **(Step 1) Introduction**

    A. Attention-gaining device

    B. Purpose

        1. Relevance Statement   *Introduction components are same as informative speech*

    C. Credibility

    D. Central Idea

II. **(Step 2) Need for Change**

    A. Reason 1

    B. Reason 2   *Include the reasons that are relevant to your audience*

    C. Reason 3

        1. Statistics (to quantify how big the problem is)

        2. Story (to put a face to the problem)

III. **(Step 3) Satisfaction**

    A. Plan (1 specific sentence of what you are asking for)

    B. How the plan works

    C. How the change will occur   *Passive agreement only*

    D. Contact info of where to go

    E. How to do it (process)   *Immediate action only*

IV. **(Step 4) Visualization of benefits**

    A. Who benefits

    B. How they benefit

    C. Analogical Reasoning (story or example)

V. **(Step 5) Conclusion**

    A. Internal summary—recap of main points

    B. Call to action/belief (one sentence that makes clear what you want the audience to do or believe)

    C. Final statement

Building Persuasive Arguments

There are a number of actions that you can take to build strong persuasive arguments. In this section, we focus on the factors that make a difference to the target audience and will help you build and convey effective persuasive messages. We will group these factors by source, message, and receiver (O'Keefe, 1990).

SOURCE FACTORS

When considering source factors, our interest centers on the "things" about the source/speaker that may make a difference to receivers. When receivers are presented with persuasive messages, what impact (if any) will source characteristics have on whether or not the persuasive message is accepted or rejected by the receivers? The following factors about the source make a difference to the receiver of a persuasive appeal:

Source Credibility

Credibility is the factor that makes the single greatest difference. Thus, the single most important thing to the receiver about the source is the credibility of the source. Receivers evaluate the credibility of a source in two ways. The lesson for speakers is to do all you can (within accepted ethical bounds) to influence how receivers judge your competence and trustworthiness. Neither are easy to establish, especially with an unfamiliar audience. There are several actions that you can take to positively influence how the audience assesses your competence and trustworthiness in a persuasive speech.

- **Competence**. Your competence as a speaker should be established in the introduction of your speech, just as you did in the introduction of your informative speech. That is, you should convey to the audience how you are linked to the topic, such as past experience or interest. You should tell your audience why you chose the topic.

- **Trustworthiness**. Trust is a reflection of your character. If the audience does not trust you, you are very unlikely to influence their views with your message. What are some ways that you can gain trust from your audience?

Talk with Your Audience—Not at Them

You want to make sure that you do not talk down to your audience or point the finger at them for not believing or doing what you are asking. Think about how you respond when someone causes you to feel like a bad person or unintelligent for holding different views. One way to avoid offending your audience in this way is by using words like "we" and "us" instead of "you." For example, saying that "we should all be concerned about the problem" is more effective than saying "you should do or not do this." It keeps you from separating yourself from your audience.

Stress Commonalities

Whenever possible, stress the commonalities that you share with audience members. Not surprisingly, people with similar experiences and views tend to be viewed more positively than people with whom we have little in common. If your audience feels that you have thought like them or felt the same way they have, they are more likely to trust you and your message. You can share your feelings or thoughts with them, showing them that you have believed the same way they have before or that you understand why they feel a certain way.

Be Sincere

It is important that the audience views you as sincere. If they do not believe that you care about their well-being they will not trust you or your message. Sometimes it is difficult to detect if someone is telling you the truth, but it is easy to sense when someone is sincere. A speaker demonstrates sincerity by showing their audience that they care about their beliefs and behaviors, even when they are different from their own. This is not always easy for a speaker since it must be a genuine consideration for others. Being sincere usually cannot be faked. While sincerity comes through in your delivery, you can also tell your audience that you understand how they feel, or understand why they think or do something. You will do this by answering audience objections.

Answer Audience Objections

Make use of two-sided arguments whenever possible in persuasive presentations. Speakers who make use of two-sided arguments are perceived by listeners as more objective and trustworthy than speakers who focus exclusively on one side of an issue. If you can communicate that you have carefully reviewed other potential solutions but are sold on one, you will be perceived as more credible.

RECEIVER FACTORS

When considering receiver factors, our interest centers on the internal qualities or characteristics of a listener that influences his/her reaction to persuasive appeals. Research suggests the following about receiver factors that make a difference when persuasion is taking place:

Contrary to popular opinion, there are no differences between females and males in regards to the likelihood of either accepting or rejecting a speaker's persuasive appeals. Early research in persuasion suggested that women were more easily persuaded than men. However, it is now clear that access to power (and not gender) is the factor that makes a difference. Simply put, those in positions of power are generally less susceptible to persuasion than those in lesser positions of power. As a speaker, learn to recognize who in the audience holds power and authority.

MESSAGE FACTORS

When considering message factors, our interest centers on the "things" that can be done to a message that may make a difference to receivers. For example, messages vary (or can be modified) in terms of organization and content.

CHAPTER 13

Organizing Arguments

Persuasive messages often include more than one appeal. That is, the speaker will use several different appeals or arguments to influence the attitudes/behaviors of receivers. When multiple persuasive appeals are used, is it more effective to put your best persuasive appeal first, last, or in the middle of the speech? Generally, it is best to start or end with your strongest appeal. There does not appear to be a benefit to placing the best appeal in the middle of the speech. The situation should influence your thinking about whether to start or end with your strongest persuasive argument. In other instances, the organization of your arguments may be influenced by the amount of background information that the audience requires to understand the appeal. For example, if you are making a persuasive argument involving the re-building of New Orleans, the audience may need to be informed of what the current levee system is designed to do. Thus, that informative content may influence how you organize your arguments.

Message Content

Messages can be modified in numerous ways. Research suggests the following about the content of persuasive messages:

- **Ask for moderate change**. When seeking to change existing attitudes or behaviors, the messages that are most effective are judged by receivers as advocating a position that is moderately different from the one currently held by receivers. If the message calls for little change, receivers tend not to see the need for any action on their part. If the message calls for great change, receivers tend to resist the message because of the magnitude of the change. A message that calls for moderate change (in the eyes of the receivers) tends to be most effective.

- **Make recommendations clear**. If the audience is uncertain about what you want them to believe and/or do, it is unlikely you will achieve your objectives.

- **Use long-term fear appeals**. Fear appeals work only as long as the receiver remains fearful. Fear tends to be a short-term state for most people. If you rely on fear appeals, the message must accomplish two ends. First, it must induce fear in the audience. Second, it must not make them so fearful that they are unable to act.

- **Use two-sided arguments**. When a speaker presents several different viewpoints followed by an explanation as to why he/she believes one to be the best, receivers view the source as more credible and competent. Including opposing arguments also helps the audience to trust you more. If you do not mention the opposing arguments they may think you are attempting to hide information from them, or it may show that you do not trust them with the information. In the eyes of the audience, this kind of argument suggests the speaker knows the issues and has considered more than one option. In research, you could find multiple opposing arguments. When this occurs, you should choose the arguments that are most relevant for influencing your specific audience. We call these more specific opposing arguments audience objections. When preparing persuasive speeches on questions of policy to gain passive agreement, most of your opposing arguments will be found in research. When preparing persuasive speeches on questions of policy to gain immediate action, you should ask yourself why your audience members would not already do what you are asking of them. When you construct arguments, you need to mention the opposing argument and immediately counteract it with your argument. Use the following example to better understand the process of narrowing and writing your own arguments.

- Specific Purpose: To persuade my audience to donate time to Salvation Army.

- Audience Objections:

  - Lack of time

  - Too strenuous

  - Lack of ability

  - Already volunteer with other organization(s)

Opposing Argument/Audience Objection ➡ Evidence for Your Argument

I know that you may be thinking that as a college student you don't have enough time to volunteer; however, according to the Salvation Army's national website, you can choose to volunteer for only four hours per month.

Using Evidence

Evidence is thought of as supporting material that is used to prove or disprove something. Speakers can make use of evidence in persuasive messages in a variety of ways. However, not all ways of using evidence are equally effective. Speakers use evidence to help support or refute a persuasive appeal. When using evidence in a persuasive presentation, consider the following:

- **Anticipate the objections listeners might have to the evidence**. If the evidence is dated, comes from a single study, or is questionable in some other fashion, prepare to overcome those objections with additional evidence (if possible). If you anticipate that the audience members have objections to the purpose that your evidence cannot overcome, you should revisit the purpose of the presentation.

- **Make use of specific evidence that is relevant to members of this audience**. Evidence should be relevant to your specific audience members rather than relevant to the population in general. As stated before, audience analysis is even more important in a persuasive speech because you are dealing with people's beliefs, values, attitudes, and behaviors.

- **Make use of novel, interesting evidence**. New evidence will generate a lasting impression. If your listeners have heard the same arguments before and have not changed their minds or behaviors, chances are hearing them in your speech will not create change. So, research carefully to find information that will create new arguments.

- **Make clear how the evidence is related to the specific purpose**. All evidence must directly relate to the purpose of the presentation and each argument you are making. In your speech you will need to explain its relevance.

Minimize your time with those who make noises instead of speaking what is good for your ears, else, they'll attune you with balderdash. Maximize your time with those who will inject into your ears a soothing sound of wisdom, for they'll set your mind on a sound reasoning path.

—Michael Bassey Johnson

REASONING

For the purpose of this course, we will define **reasoning** as the way people draw conclusions from the available information and evidence. We reason every day to better understand and explain why things happen. Reasoning impacts persuasive speaking in two ways. First, the speaker develops a persuasive argument that is based on some form of reasoning. Second, receivers employ reasoning in the process of accepting or rejecting a persuasive appeal. Thus, the way you and your audience reason will impact the extent to which you achieve your objectives. As a persuasive speaker, it is essential that you convince audience members to agree with your line of reasoning. In this course, we will expect you to become familiar with four methods of reasoning.

Causal Reasoning

When individuals use causal reasoning, they draw the conclusion that a cause (often the presence of something or some act) leads to a specific effect or set of effects. For example, a driver involved in a minor accident might conclude that the presence of a deer on the road caused an accident. The driver might further reason that if the cause (the deer) had not been present, the effect (hitting a tree) would not have occurred.

- Because a deer ran in front of my car, I swerved to avoid it and hit a tree.

Analogical Reasoning

When individuals employ analogical reasoning, they draw conclusions based on comparisons. For example, if you are a great public speaker, you would make a great political candidate. Reasoning by comparison suggests that many things in our world are believed to be associated. In a question of policy speech, you may use analogical reasoning to show your audience where a similar plan to yours has worked successfully (visualization step in Monroe's Motivational Sequence).

- Many have already enrolled in this exercise program and benefited greatly. If it worked for them, it can work for you too.

Reasoning from Specific Instance

The use of this type of reasoning suggests that a person is making use of specific facts to draw a much broader conclusion about others or events in the world. You must find the conclusion that is being drawn in the statement. It could come in the beginning or end but it will be very general and vague. When you eliminate the conclusion, examine what is left. If everything left are facts, it is reasoning from specific instance.

- Pollution is present in the Tennessee River at Knoxville. Pollution is present in the Tennessee River at Chattanooga. Therefore, the Tennessee River is polluted.

Reasoning from Principle

This type of reasoning suggests that a person applies a general premise (principle) to arrive at a very specific conclusion. For the most part, reasoning from principle lacks the hard facts found in reasoning from specific instance. However, many times it will include a three-fold statement that begins with a general principle followed by a minor premise that may resemble a fact and ends with a specific conclusion. Again, no matter what the wording, the conclusion is what you must find. If after eliminating the conclusion not everything left are facts, it is reasoning from principle.

- I think arthritis runs in my family. I will probably suffer from it like my sister has.

- Politicians who are guilty of corruption do not deserve to be reelected. Last year our U.S. representative was found to be corrupt by using campaign donations for personal finance gain. Therefore, our U.S. representatives do not deserve to be reelected.

Notice when you take away the conclusion in the above examples you are left with either no facts at all or a fact and a premise like the second example above.

PREMISE ⟹ FACT ⟹ SPECIFIC CONCLUSION

The components will not always be in this order, but notice that it is different from specific instance in that, if you take out the conclusion being drawn, you are not left with facts only.

CHAPTER 13

DISTINGUISHING BETWEEN THE FOUR TYPES OF REASONING

Distinguishing between the four types of reasoning is difficult if you do not use the following process of elimination. The following information explains how to distinguish between the four types:

Use a process of elimination and begin with causal reasoning. If it does not include both a cause and an effect in the statement (A caused B to occur), you can move on. Next, attempt to eliminate analogical reasoning (analogy). This is where two cases/situations are being compared, and claims that what happens for the first item will happen for the second because of their similarities. If you can eliminate causal and analogy, you are left with the two most difficult types of reasoning to differentiate: specific instance and principle. The first thing to do is to find the conclusion that is being drawn. The conclusion could be at the beginning or end of the statement. Eliminate the conclusion being drawn and evaluate what is left. If all of what is left is a fact or multiple facts, then it is specific instance. If facts are absent completely or only a portion of what is left is a fact, then it is reasoning from principle. Again, the conclusion is what you are looking for in the statement. As a back-up method, look at the nature of the conclusion. If the conclusion that is being drawn is very broad, general, or vague, it is reasoning from specific instance. If the conclusion being drawn is specific in nature, it is principle. Make sure that you spend time completing the reasoning activity from the back section of the text and obtain the correct answers from your instructor to study.

Reasoning Limitations

All forms of reasoning have limitations. How would you describe the limitations of the four methods of reasoning described above? If you are unsure what the limitations are, consider the following:

- Causal reasoning is limited to the extent that we have identified accurately the cause(s) that lead to specific effects. Recall our example involving a traffic accident. In addition to the presence of water on the road, would the speed of the vehicle (in combination with the water on the road) impact the car leaving the road? Thus, it is often difficult to sort out clearly all of the causes and all of the effects.

- Analogical reasoning is limited to the extent that comparisons hold true. If people enjoy watching college basketball, does that mean they will enjoy watching professional basketball?

- Reasoning from a specific instance is limited to the extent that facts from several specific instances can be applied to a more general class of events or others. In other words, because the information is true in two or three instances, is it true in all or most all instances?

- Reasoning from a principle is limited to the extent that we can apply a broad idea or principle to a specific instance. In other words, because we conclude that the information is true in most all cases, is it true in this case?

FALLACIES

Effective speakers tend to be more aware of the limitations associated with each type of reasoning and are cautious about how they make use of reasoning in the development of persuasive presentations. Far too often, however, speakers employ incorrect reasoning, or reasoning that is not sound in their persuasive speech. A **fallacy** involves errors in reasoning. The eight fallacies are explained below.

Hasty Generalization

This type of reasoning error occurs when a speaker jumps to a general conclusion on the basis of poorly selected specific facts. To avoid this, seek out other evidence such as statistics or testimony to support your broad conclusion.

- She has been wearing really baggy clothes lately. She must be pregnant.

Mistaken Cause

For all of us, one experience (for example, a paper assignment) is always followed by other experiences (leaving the classroom, talking with friends, and so on). Reasoning errors involving mistaken causes occur when a speaker erroneously assumes that the first event/experience must have caused the second event/experience.

- Andy would not loan me his notes and so I failed the exam.

Invalid Analogy

An invalid analogy takes place when a speaker uses fallacious reasoning to suggest similarities in two cases when they are truly different.

- How could raising a child be any different from taking care of a pet? All you have to do is feed it, give it shelter, and try to keep it safe.

Red Herring

Speakers seeking to divert attention from the issue at hand often engage in fallacious reasoning by introducing irrelevant issues into the topic of discussion.

- Why should we be concerned with Siberian tigers becoming extinct when there are more and more homeless people who need our support?

Ad Hominem (Latin for "Against the Man")

Simply put, a speaker uses fallacious reasoning by attacking the messenger rather than the message or idea that is in dispute.

- You can't possibly support Senator Smith's position on gun control. He's an untrustworthy idiot.

CHAPTER 13

False Dilemma

A false dilemma involves a situation where the speaker uses fallacious reasoning to force listeners to choose between only two alternatives when more than two alternatives exist. It is usually presented as an ultimatum.

- Our university must either raise student tuition or cut operating budgets of all departments on campus.

Bandwagon

Bandwagon reasoning is fallacious because it does not concern the soundness of an idea. This form of fallacious reasoning is based on the notion that because something is popular it is therefore correct, good, or desired.

- You should buy TeethWhite. Nine out of ten dentists recommend this toothpaste to their patients.

Slippery Slope

Conclusions that are based on an illogical chain of events often involve slippery slope reasoning. A speaker engaging in slippery slope reasoning assumes that the first step will be followed by other steps that cannot be prevented.

- If I don't make an A on this assignment, then I will not do well in this course, and I probably won't get into law school and will probably never amount to very much.

EMOTIONAL APPEALS

Since the work of Aristotle, study and instruction in public speaking has suggested that emotion plays a key role in persuasive speaking. This view is grounded in the idea that people are more likely to change attitudes or behaviors when their passions are stirred. In your persuasive speech you may consider making your audience feel sad, proud, angry, sympathetic, fearful, obligated, and so on to further influence them. What emotions do you need your audience to feel in order for their beliefs or actions to change? You do not, however, want to abuse emotional appeal. The key is to never substitute emotional appeal for evidence or reasoning, but use it in addition to solid evidence and reasoning.

Managing Receiver Emotions

Effective persuasive speakers recognize the importance of managing the emotions of the receivers. There is no single method to ensure that, as a speaker, you generate the desired emotional response in receivers. However, the following factors are often used to influence emotional states of listeners:

- **Language use.** Vivid, descriptive language is often used to elicit emotional responses from the audience. Often, this is accomplished in the form of an example, story, or personal experience.

- **Nonverbal messages.** Facial expressions and body movement convey to an audience the mood the speaker is attempting to establish.

- **Use of voice.** Volume, vocal variety, and pauses are used by speakers to convey more than content or nonverbal cues.

Persuasive speakers often employ appeals that are based, in part, on managing the emotional state of the receivers in terms of fear, or anger, or sympathy. While the emotional states of receivers are important in persuasive speaking, consider the following:

- The effects of emotion on attitudes or behaviors tend to persist as long as the emotional state persists. When the receiver gets over the feelings of fear, guilt, or happiness, the effects on attitudes tend to go away.

- How ethical is it to make others angry or guilty or fearful? Are there situations where it would be both appropriate and ethical to generate strong emotions in receivers? Are there instances where it is inappropriate? When answering this, consider the major rule above. One way that emotional appeal is abused is when a persuasive speech relies solely upon emotional appeal and uses it as a substitute for evidence and reasoning. This is not only unethical, but your audience will recognize your attempt to take advantage of them.

Key Terms/Concepts to Know

Persuasion definition

Target Audience Attitude Change Model

Target audience

Questions of fact

Questions of value

Questions of policy

Monroe's motivational sequence

Building persuasive arguments

Source factors

Receiver factors

Message factors

Reasoning

Fallacies

Emotional appeals

Reference List

Adapted from McKerrow, R.E., Gronbeck, B.E., Ehninger, D., & Monroe, A.H. (2000). *Principles and types of speech communication* (14th ed.). New York: Addison Wesley Longman, Inc.

O'Keefe, D. (1990). *Persuasion*. Newbury Park: Sage.

CHAPTER 13

STUDENT NOTES

CHAPTER 14

SPECIAL OCCASION SPEAKING

CHAPTER OBJECTIVES

This chapter is designed to help you understand:

- The process of preparing and delivering a special occasion speech

- To understand the different types of special event speeches

Many special occasions call for different types of speeches. There are five main types of special occasion speeches. For many special occasions, more than one type of speech may be appropriate. Special occasion speeches differ considerably from informative or persuasive speeches. In fact, each type of special occasion speech calls for different kinds of preparation and delivery. When preparing a special occasion speech, consider factors such as the purpose of the event, its location, and the composition of the audience.

Guidelines for Special Occasion Speeches

No matter the occasion, the following guidelines will assist you if you are asked to speak at a special event.

BE CREATIVE

Special occasion speeches are generally one part of a larger event. Events such as weddings, retirements, or funerals will require the speaker to adopt objectives that are quite different from more conventional speaking events. For example, a special occasion speech may involve objectives such as entertaining or comforting rather than informing or persuading. Special event speeches will require more vivid language use along with discussions of personal experiences.

They may also involve unconventional visual aids. Your success in achieving the desired speaking objectives hinges, in part, on how creative you are as a speaker.

ADAPT THE SPEECH TO THE OCCASION

A special occasion speech must be adapted to the occasion. Is the occasion a small, informal barbecue outdoors or a large, formal banquet indoors? What is the attire at this event? Often, situational factors of the occasion will give the speaker clues as to how to proceed. An informal event will call for less formal language and delivery than a formal event. Based on where the event is held, you may need a podium for a formal occasion or you may be expected to stand in front of your audience during less formal occasions.

ADAPT THE SPEECH TO THE AUDIENCE

Consider why the audience is in attendance. Does this occasion require the audience to be here or did they choose to be here? This will help you prepare for the speech and determine what would be appropriate or inappropriate.

ORGANIZE THE INFORMATION

A belief held by many is that a special occasion speech requires no preparation or concern for organization. It is a speech that is delivered "off the cuff" so to speak. This belief is wrong—special occasion speeches must also be well organized. For this kind of speech, topical and chronological patterns of organizing are often the most useful when preparing and delivering special occasion speeches.

MAINTAIN DIRECT EYE CONTACT

Eye contact is even more important for special occasion speeches because most events call for less formality than scholarly presentations.

USE VOICE/BODY EFFECTIVELY

The speaker's voice in a special occasion speech must be especially engaging for the audience. All of the dimensions of voice such as volume, vocal variety, rate, and pauses must be used in concert.

While the guidelines above apply to all special event speeches, there are unique characteristics associated with the different types of special event speeches. Below we will briefly review five different types of special event speeches.

Speeches of Introduction

One type of special occasion speech is a speech of introduction. The purpose of this speech is to introduce a main speaker or performer to the audience. Keep in mind that the audience is not there to see/hear you but the person/group you are introducing. If you are asked to deliver this type of speech, you must be well-informed about the individual or group that is introduced. Preparation is one key to an effective speech of introduction.

SPEECH OF INTRODUCTION GUIDELINES

Build Enthusiasm for the Upcoming Speaker/Performer
Seek to generate audience interest and excitement regarding the individual or group that you are introducing. One way you can do this is by giving your audience information that they may not have ever heard about this person/group. Be creative in finding information. Consider including information regarding achievements, personal struggles, family information, and career path.

Build Enthusiasm for the Speaker's Topic
Not only will you need to include information about the speaker/performer, you should also clarify what this person/group is speaking about. If you are introducing a speaker, clarify for the audience what his or her topic will be. If you are introducing a group, such as a band, clarify what they will perform.

Establish a Welcoming Climate that Boosts the Speaker's Credibility
Seek to make use of information that gives the speaker/performer credibility appropriate for the audience. Depending on whom you are introducing, your remarks to boost their credibility may differ. Avoid any information that might embarrass the person/group and call into question their credibility.

Make Sure Your Remarks Are Accurate
When finding information for your speech of introduction, make certain that the dates are correct, the stories are true, and the events are factual. Your credibility as a speaker and the person's/group's credibility may be destroyed by inaccurate information.

Adapt Your Remarks to the Main Speaker
You must always take the speaker into account when preparing your speech of introduction. For example, you would not include the same information in a speech introducing the CEO of a company that you would in a speech introducing a comedian.

Adapt Your Remarks to the Audience
When considering what to include in your speech and how to deliver it, consider the audience. What type of person would be at this event? What do they know about this speaker/performer? What would they be interested in hearing or learning about the person/group? As discussed earlier, consider why they are there. Is attendance required or voluntary?

Create a Sense of Anticipation and Drama
One way that you can build enthusiasm for the upcoming speaker is to wait and reveal the speaker's/performer's name at the very end of the speech. You may also want to organize your speech in a fashion that will build upon importance of content from the introduction to conclusion.

Adhere to Time Limits

Remember that the audience did not come to this event to see you but rather to see the speaker/performer. Therefore, the speech of introduction is much shorter than other types of speeches. The appropriate speech length for a speech of introduction in this class will be two to three minutes. Speeches of introduction have been known to be shorter for some occasions. The length of the speech is sometimes determined by how much the audience already knows about the speaker/performer.

Commemorative Speeches

The purpose of a commemorative speech is to inspire the audience by paying tribute to a person, a group of people, an institution, or an idea. They usually represent milestones in someone's life, such as an anniversary, birthday, graduation commencement, retirement ceremony or the beginning or end of something such as a eulogy at a funeral, the christening of a ship, or a groundbreaking ceremony. A best man's speech at a wedding would be considered a commemorative speech only if the purpose is to pay tribute to the bride and groom while inspiring the audience. If the speaker is there to entertain the audience, it would be considered an after-dinner speech. Below are examples of specific purpose statements for commemorative speeches:

- To inspire my audience to pursue their dreams, by paying tribute to my mother at her funeral.

- To inspire my audience to build on our success, by paying tribute to a retiring company president.

COMMEMORATIVE SPEECH GUIDELINES

Use an Introduction that Captures the Spirit of the Event

Begin your commemorative speech with an introduction that gains attention first and then introduces what or who you are paying tribute to. Stories about the person being honored that capture the spirit of the event are often useful when starting the introduction. Keep in mind that the story should be both impactful and brief.

Use Supporting Material that Inspires

Since the purpose is to inspire your audience, find material for your speech that meets that goal. Vivid language is important to inspire your audience, as well as finding material that will evoke emotions among members of the audience.

Use a Conclusion that Captures the Spirit of the Event

Just as in the introduction, consider closing the speech with a story about the main speaker that is both impactful and brief. Close with a vivid, memorable statement that unifies the overall theme of your speech. Remember: end your speech with a bang!

After-Dinner Speeches

The purpose of an after-dinner speech is to entertain the audience by making thoughtful comments about a topic in a lighthearted manner. This type of speech does not have to be made after dinner, or even relate to meals or food. Unlike other special occasion speeches, this kind of speech is organized around a topic. However, the goal is to entertain your audience. You can take any topic and create a specific purpose for either an informative, persuasive, or after-dinner speech shown in the following example:

Topic: Intercollegiate Athletics

- **Informative Specific Purpose:** To inform my audience of the current state of intercollegiate athletics.

- **Persuasive Specific Purpose:** To persuade my audience to support changes to the governance of intercollegiate athletics.

- **After-Dinner Specific Purpose:** To entertain my audience by sharing with them the confusing rules that govern intercollegiate athletics.

The following is another example of an after-dinner speech purpose:

- **Specific Purpose:** To entertain my audience by discussing some of the strange traditions associated with college sports.

AFTER-DINNER SPEECH GUIDELINES

Choose an Appropriate Topic for the Audience
The speaker must select a topic that is of interest to the audience and the occasion.

The Introduction
Just as in a commemorative speech, begin your after-dinner speech with an introduction that gains attention first and introduces your topic/purpose. Once again, stories are an effective way of gaining attention and relating the topic to the audience.

Use Supporting Material that Entertains
Since the purpose is to entertain the audience, find material for your speech that meets that goal. Conduct research on the topic to find its "lighter side." Seek interesting information that will keep the audience's attention.

Use Tasteful Humor
Some speakers attempt to entertain their audience by using humor. However, humor does not have to be included in the speech in order for you to meet your goal. Make use of humor if it comes naturally to you and it is not something that you have to force. If humor does not come naturally to you, the audience may feel uncomfortable with its

use and be uncertain as to whether or not they should laugh. Most often, it will be funny because of the supporting material itself. When using humor, make certain that your target audience will find it tasteful. Do not offend your audience!

The Conclusion
Just as you did in your informative and persuasive speeches, it is necessary to end with a vivid, memorable statement that unifies the overall theme of your speech. Remember to end your speech with a bang!

Adhere to Time Limits
An after-dinner speech is not an impromptu speech. Rather, the speaker was invited in advance to deliver an after-dinner speech. The speaker should check with the host to determine the time expectations for the speech.

Speech of Presentation
The purpose of a speech of presentation is to recognize someone with a gift, an award, or some other form of public recognition. It is usually shorter than other types of special occasion speeches because the audience is waiting to hear from the person receiving the recognition. The goal here is not to review all of the events in the life of the person receiving the gift or award, but rather to simply explain why the person is receiving it.

Speech of Acceptance
The purpose of a speech of acceptance is to give thanks for a gift, an award, or some other form of public recognition. This may include thanking the person(s) who presented the gift or award and the people that helped to make it possible. Although a speech of acceptance is usually longer than a speech of presentation, it should be brief.

Key Terms/Concepts to Know

Guidelines for special occasion speeches

Speeches of introduction

Commemorative speeches

After-dinner speeches

Speech of presentation

Speech of acceptance